Wallens

A "Down and Dirty" Guide to Theology

Other Books by Donald K. McKim

The Church: Its Early Life

The Authority and Interpretation of the Bible: An Historical Approach (with Jack B. Rogers)

The Authoritative Word: Essays on the Nature of Scripture (editor)

Readings in Calvin's Theology (editor)

What Christians Believe about the Bible

A Guide to Contemporary Hermeneutics: Major Trends in Biblical Interpretation (editor)

How Karl Barth Changed My Mind (editor)

Ramism in William Perkins' Theology

Theological Turning Points: Major Issues in Christian Thought

Major Themes in the Reformed Tradition (editor)

Encyclopedia of the Reformed Faith (editor)

Kerygma: The Bible and Theology (4 volumes)

The Bible in Theology and Preaching

Westminster Dictionary of Theological Terms

God Never Forgets: Faith, Hope, and Alzheimer's Disease (editor)

Historical Handbook of Major Biblical Interpreters (editor)

Historical Dictionary of Reformed Churches (with Robert Benedetto and Darrell L. Guder)

Calvin's Institutes: *Abridged Edition* (editor)

Introducing the Reformed Faith: Biblical Revelation, Christian Tradition, Contemporary Significance

The Westminster Handbook to Reformed Theology (editor)

The Cambridge Companion to Martin Luther (editor)

Presbyterian Beliefs: A Brief Introduction

Presbyterian Questions, Presbyterian Answers

The Cambridge Companion to John Calvin (editor)

Calvin and the Bible (editor)

Historical Dictionary of Reformed Churches, 2nd ed. (with Robert Benedetto)

Dictionary of Major Biblical Interpreters (editor)

Ever a Vision: A Brief History of Pittsburgh Theological Seminary, 1959-2009

A Reformed Faith That Lives Today (Japanese translation)

More Presbyterian Questions, More Presbyterian Answers

A "Down and Dirty" Guide to Theology

Donald K. McKim

WESTMINSTER
JOHN KNOX PRESS
LOUISVILLE • KENTUCKY

First edition
Published by Westminster John Knox Press
Louisville, Kentucky

11 12 13 14 15 16 17 18 19 20—10 9 8 7 6 5 4 3 2 1

Book design by James Satter
Interior illustrations by Ron Hill, www.RonHillArtist.com
Cover design by Mark Abrams
Cover illustration by Ron Hill, www.RonHillArtist.com

Library of Congress Cataloging-in-Publication Data

McKim, Donald K.
  A "down and dirty" guide to theology / Donald K. McKim.—1st ed.
    p. cm.
  Includes bibliographical references.
  ISBN 978-0-664-23405-8 (alk. paper)
 1. Theology.   I. Title.
 BR118.M29   2011
 230—dc23

                                              2011019194

PRINTED IN THE UNITED STATES OF AMERICA

♾ The paper used in this publication meets the minimum requirements
of the American National Standard for Information Sciences—
Permanence of Paper for Printed Library Materials, ANSI Z39.48-1992.

Westminster John Knox Press advocates the responsible
use of our natural resources. The text paper of this book
is made from 30% post-consumer waste.

Most Westminster John Knox Press books are available at special
quantity discounts when purchased in bulk by corporations,
organizations, and special-interest groups. For more
information, please e-mail SpecialSales@wjkbooks.com.

For my family—

LindaJo
Stephen and Caroline, and Maddie
Karl and Lauren

—with gratitude and joy in our lives and love together

CONTENTS

V. THEOLOGY AND . . .

VI. A BIT OF HISTORY

VII. DOING THEOLOGY

VIII. THEOLOGY TODAY

IX. THE PERSONAL TOUCH

X. GOING ON FROM HERE

A FINAL WORD

PREFACE

I hope this is a book for you! It is if you have any interest at all in Christian theology.

When you hear the word "theology," you may yawn. It sounds like a boring, technical discussion about questions people worried about long ago. "Theology" may not inspire much enthusiasm.

I hope this book can change that. It is a "down and dirty" guide to theology, especially for those for whom theology is a new topic for study. This book is for people who have no background in studying theology. It is for Christians in churches who wonder about words and ideas they hear about week in and week out. It is for those who are beginning theological study, perhaps in a seminary or divinity school, or in a college or university. The book will be of interest to seminary graduates or pastors who want to think again about some of the "basics" they have learned before. It is also a book for the curious—for those who wonder what Christian theology is about, how it is understood, and what its main directions are. I hope this book can help make theology come alive today!

The following "sketch" for inquisitive and interested people tries to say a bit about some important elements in theological study. This is not an introduction to theology in a formal sense. Rather, it is a series of orienting perspectives to give a snapshot of some key dimensions of Christian theology, at a basic level. The lens is wide angle—a number of subjects pop up here that will not find their way into regular introductory theology books. I hope these topics are helpful and interesting. This is a book to dip into during spare few minutes or when you need a break. It is a book with things to ponder and to enjoy.

I have a passion for sharing theological ideas. I try to do this through writing, teaching, and service to the church. My perspectives on the nature of theology and interesting dimensions of theology are shaped by the many influences I have imbibed. I have set down some things I see as important for those setting sail on theological seas. I hope the scattered topics will be a useful guide toward further study. As the national motto of Spain puts it, "*Plus ultra*"—there is "more beyond"!

The book is written as simply as possible. A number of bullet points indicate major thoughts. They direct the way to ideas that can be developed further in some of the fine theological resources we have access to today. (A list of some of these resources for further study is included.) This book is a sampler. It covers some of the topics that find their way into the study of theology. I draw from a variety of sources. My perspective is just one vision among many. But here is a preliminary sketch—a "baptism by sprinkling," if you will. This book simply opens the doors and windows.

The illustrations help some of these ideas be more memorable—and fun! Theology has been called the "joyful science." So touches of humor and a few laughs along the way are most appropriate.

My hope is that this book can help inspire us to move beyond "yawns"' to engaging theological ideas. The Christian church has lived by its theological insights for centuries. It has developed and used a vocabulary to describe its understandings: of God, Jesus Christ, salvation, the life to come, and much else. This book tries to unpack some of these ideas in a very basic way, introduce characters who have been important, and provide orientation to the kinds of questions theologians and the church have found to be most significant.

For us, the question is the one found in the book of Ezekiel: "Can these bones live?" (Ezek. 37:3). Can these "old bones"— theological terms, personalities, questions—"live" for us today; can they influence our lives today?

I welcome you to these pages and to this "down and dirty" guide to theology!

ACKNOWLEDGMENTS

All books reflect the combined influences of many people. These are filtered through the work of a single author.

The theological influences on me through the decades have been many and significant. Reading, listening, learning, talking—all form the person of the theologian.

I would like to thank Ron Hill for his great illustrations.

As always, my family is God's great blessing to me: LindaJo has been my loving wife through our married years and our theological journeys together. Our son Stephen and his wife, Caroline, and daughter, Maddie, are loved beyond words, as are our son Karl and his wife, Lauren, whose lives together we celebrate with great joy. For our family, I am immeasurably thankful. This book is dedicated to them.

I am grateful to my teachers of theology, especially Jack Rogers and Arthur Cochrane. All have imparted to me important glimpses of the gracious God.

I. WHAT'S IT ALL ABOUT?

1. WHAT IS THEOLOGY?

"Theology" is the study of God. It comes from two Greek words: *theos*, "God," and *logos*, "study of." As "biology" is the study of *bios* ("life"), "psychology" is the study of the psyche, and "zoology" is the study of zoos—make that animals—so "theology" is the study of God.

That's a tall order, isn't it? When we think about such a thing, a number of questions arise: Is there a God? How is this God to be known? Is this a God who is active in human history and human lives?

The subject (or object) of theology makes it unique. Like any other discipline, theology should be studied by using the methods that are appropriate to what is being studied. We use experiments and laboratories to study chemistry, for example. But how to study theology? How do you find a way to study "God"—an idea or, perhaps, a "person," who by definition is beyond all human apprehension or thought?

In the Christian tradition, the living God is understood as the one to whom theology looks. We are dealing with a living being. This is a God who speaks, who acts, who is personal, and who is over and beyond all humans in greatness and power. "Studying" a God like this is a daunting but potentially wonderful task.

One of my favorite definitions of theology comes from the old-time Puritan theologian William Perkins (1558–1602). He wrote that "theologie is the science of living blessedly for ever. Blessed life arises from the knowledge of God."* Christians maintain that our best life possible is one that is lived in relationship with the living God. The "blessed life" is based on the "knowledge of God." It is this knowledge that theology helps to provide.

* William Perkins, "A Golden Chaine," in *The Workes of William Perkins,* 3 vols. (Cambridge: John Legate, 1616–1618), I:11.

2. GOALS OF THEOLOGY

The study of theology is approached in many ways. If you read books written by contemporary theologians, you will find that they are concerned with a wide range of topics. They approach their theological work with a variety of methods. They have different presuppositions in their work. There is not one single "theology" that unites all theologians or Christian believers.

For Christian theologians, the goals of theology can emerge in different ways, with individual theologians placing emphases in different places. But in a broad sense, Christian theologians—or Christians who are seeking to learn more about God—have three important focuses or goals for theological study. These are set forth by Geoffrey Wainwright, a British Methodist theologian:

- **Worship.** Theology conveys a Christian vision of God—who God is and what God has done. Worship is "the place in which that vision comes to a sharp focus, a concentrated expression, and it is here that the vision has often been found to be at its most appealing. The theologian's thinking therefore properly draws on the worship of the Christian community and is in duty bound to contribute to it."[*]

- **Doctrine.** A goal of theology is the "coherent intellectual expression of the Christian vision."[†] This leads the theologian to express views about the church's worship and theological language while also being concerned to communicate Christian teachings or doctrines to those who do not yet believe the Christian message or share the Christian vision.

[*] Geoffrey Wainwright, *Doxology: The Praise of God in Worship, Doctrine, and Life* (New York: Oxford University Press, 1980), 3.
[†] Ibid.

- **Life.** The theologian is concerned with the world God loves and seeks to communicate the Christian vision within the lives of everyday people. The Christian theologian proposes to the Christian community "the most effective ways of allowing its vision to illuminate and transform reality to the advantage of all humanity."[*]

Those who study Christian theology as "theologians" will continually be involved in these three goals, in various dimensions and in a variety of ways. They may do this as "professional" theologians, in different contexts, or simply as members of a Christian church who are seeking to "grow in the grace and knowledge of our Lord and Savior Jesus Christ" (2 Pet. 3:18). These "goals" form the web in which our Christian lives are lived out. The study of theology leads us to attend to them all and to commit ourselves as Christian theologians to communicating our theological understandings.

[*] Ibid., 4.

3. THEOLOGY: THE JOYFUL SCIENCE

"Make a joyful noise to the Lord, all the earth" (Ps. 100:1). So begins one of the most well-known psalms.

When we think of what this means, we usually think of worship. In corporate worship, the Christian community gathers to sing praises, to glorify, to make a "joyful noise" to the Lord, the God of the Scriptures who has called the community of faith together.

But what if there are other ways of expressing and entering into joy? What if doing theology is one of these ways? What if theology is a "joyful science"?

This was what the theologian Karl Barth believed. He said theology is "a peculiarly beautiful science. Indeed, we can confidently say that it is the most beautiful of all the sciences." Barth believed that the theologian who does not find joy in theological work "is not a theologian at all."* Theology is "a singularly beautiful and joyful science, so that it is only willingly and cheerfully or not at all that we can be theologians."†

Why is theology so beautiful? Theology is beautiful because the subject and the object of theology is the living God. The God we encounter in the Bible, who has been revealed supremely in Jesus Christ, is the God to whom the "whole earth" should make a "joyful noise." This God radiates joy. This God is beautiful. This God is the God of glory, and, says Barth, "it is a glory that awakens joy, and is itself joyful."‡

In our worship, in our theology, in all we are and do, we are invited to share in this glory of God, to participate in the

* Karl Barth, *Church Dogmatics*, II/1, ed. G. W. Bromiley and T. F. Torrance (Edinburgh: T. & T. Clark, 1964), 656.
† Karl Barth, *Church Dogmatics*, IV/3, ed. G. W. Bromiley and T. F. Torrance (Edinburgh: T. & T. Clark, 1992), 881.
‡ Barth, *CD* II/1, 655.

life of God, and to be in relationship with God in Jesus Christ. This is the Christian message. At the birth of Jesus Christ, the angels brought "good news of great joy for all the people" (Luke 2:10). The earth shares in the glory of God in Jesus Christ; theologians share in the glory of God in Jesus Christ—and this means joy!

Theologians have the inestimable privilege—by God's grace and the deepest pleasure—to be able to study, contemplate, live, and enjoy the great glory of God, as God is revealed to us in the Scriptures and in Jesus Christ. This is the greatest joy imaginable. It is the most wonderful life imaginable—to be able to *know* the great God of glory: "The heavens are telling the glory of God; and the firmament proclaims his handiwork" (Ps. 19:1). In God's presence there is "fullness of joy" (Ps. 16:11).

Theology is the joyful science because it has to do with God. This is the God who is "good" and whose "steadfast love endures forever" (Ps. 100:5). No wonder the psalmist could also exclaim, "O come, let us sing to the Lord; let us make a joyful noise to the rock of our salvation" (Ps. 95:1). We sing and worship and pray and serve and "do theology" to the good God who is our "exceeding joy" (Ps. 43:4).

II. THEOLOGIANS

4. WHO IS A THEOLOGIAN?

If theology is the study of God, then anyone who says something about God is a theologian. We can't escape it. From a prayer we pray, to a conversation we have, to speaking the name of God casually or in a curse—all of these are ways of mentioning or recognizing God. Thus, they make the one who is focusing on God a theologian.

The dictionary defines a theologian as a "specialist in theology." This is true in the more precise sense. But insofar as any of us—no matter who we are—has something to say about God, something to ask about God, something to claim about God, we are being theologians.

If the Bible is right and the Christian church is right that God is a "living God," then any statements about this God involve us in some kind of relationship with God. We may praise God, or love God, or complain to God, or curse God, or even deny God's existence. But in any and all these activities, we are still dealing with God in some way. If there is a God, and that God is a living God, then all our statements and all our feelings and all our sense of who we are draws us into a relationship with this God in some form or fashion.

If this is so, then the next questions will be these: Who is this God? What is God like? How do we know God? What kind of relationship might we have with God? These are the questions that the study of theology deals with when it is carried out by scholars and in Christian churches. Will we be *self-conscious* theologians, or will we be *unreflective* theologians? Will we seek ways to find out more about this God? Or will we live life as "one darn thing after another," never seeking to reflect upon or study or learn of God, never seeking a knowledge of God that just might make a difference in what we think and believe and on how we live?

A View from Liberation Theologians

Two Latin American theologians associated with the approach to theology known as liberation theology have written well about who is a theologian:

All members of the people of God think about their faith: all of them, not only the professionals, "do" theology in a way. There can, indeed, be no faith without a minimum of theology. How so? Because faith is human and involves a "longing to understand"—*fides quaerens intellectum*—as the classic theologians put it. All who believe want to understand something of their faith. And as soon as you think about faith, you are already doing theology. So all Christians are in a certain sense theologians, and become more so the more they think about their faith. The subject of faith is the subject of theology—thinking and thought-out faith, cultivated collectively in the bosom of the church. The base communities,[*] trying to draw lessons for today from the pages of the Gospel, are "doing" theology, theologizing. Furthermore, popular theology is thinking about the faith in solidarity: all give their opinions, completing or correcting those of others, each helping the other to assimilate the matter more clearly. Or is it that laypersons have no right to think? Are they just the "learning church," the taught church, and in no way the educating and educative church?[†]

You don't need an academic degree to be a theologian!

* "Base communities" refers to small groups of Christian laypersons, particularly among the rural poor, who meet together to try to understand their day-to-day life in light of Christian faith.

† Leonardo and Clodovis Boff, *Introducing Liberation Theology* (Maryknoll, NY: Orbis Books, 1987), 16.

5. THEOLOGY FOR EVERYONE

Everyone who has to do with God in any way is a theologian. All our statements about God are theological statements. When we reflect on God, wonder about God, or even seek to disprove in our own minds that God exists, we are engaged in theology—we are involved with God, either explicitly or implicitly.

This means that theology is for everyone. Everyone on earth can—and should—think and reflect on God, seek to study God, seek to know God. Everyone should be a theologian.

This is certainly true in the Christian sense. The God Christians worship and seek to serve is the living God. We know of this God through the Bible. God is a God who wants to be made known to the world and to all its people. Christians believe God has been revealed, that God has communicated God's self to the world. The clearest and most definitive revelation of God is in the person of Jesus Christ. Christians believe Jesus of Nazareth, a Palestinian Jew, is the one person who most fully and decisively has conveyed the reality of God to us human beings. Jesus, Christians believe, provides the way for us to know who God is and to have a relationship with God.

So just as theology is for everyone, Jesus Christ is for everyone. The Scriptures connect God's sending Jesus Christ into the world with God's love: "For God so loved the world that he gave his only Son, so that everyone who believes in him may not perish but may have eternal life" (John 3:16). God sent Jesus Christ into the world because God loves the world. God wants the world to know God, and the world can know God by knowing Jesus Christ.

So theology is for everyone. Everyone can learn of God, can study about God, and come to know God in Jesus Christ.

There are, of course, specialists in theology—persons we call "theologians." But from the simplest theological statement— "God is love" (1 John 4:8)—to the most complicated theological book, theology is open to all. God calls us, God invites us, to learn of God, to know God, and to "grow in the knowledge of God" (Col. 1:10).

We can study theology at any depth and at any level. But through it all, theology is for everyone!

6. TASKS OF THE THEOLOGIAN

"Theology begins with wonder and with unanswered questions."* So said Avery Cardinal Dulles, one of the great recent Roman Catholic theologians.

If this is so, then theologians have big tasks, don't they? The "wonder" at the beginning is wonder at God, who is both the subject and the object of theology. Theology is about God. In the face of God, what else can we do but wonder? God is over and beyond us (transcendent, as the theologians say) but also with us (imminent, particularly in Jesus Christ and through the Holy Spirit). In the face of who God is—as we know God from the Scriptures—we join all biblical writers who praise and glorify God. The psalmist proclaims, "Great is the Lord, and greatly to be praised; his greatness is unsearchable" (Ps. 145:3).

Naturally, in the face of this God of wonder, we do have unanswered questions: What is God like? How can we know God? Who are we as humans? What does the future hold? These and many more lodge in our minds.

In some way, the task of theologians is both to proclaim who God is and to address our human questions. In different ways, theologians have emphasized each aspect of this overall task. Some have stressed theology's role in proclaiming the "mystery" of God (1 Tim. 3:16); others have focused on the deep human questions that baffle us. Both are important and belong to the work of the theologian.

Dulles was more specific when he wrote that theology is "a methodical effort to articulate the truth implied in Christian faith, the faith of the Church."† We know something about the great wonder and mystery of God, since Christian

* Avery Dulles, *The Craft of Theology: From Symbol to System* (New York: Crossroad, 1992), 11.
† Ibid., 8.

faith understands that God has been revealed through the Scriptures and specifically in Jesus Christ. "Within the Bible the figure of Jesus Christ stands out as God's supreme self-disclosure," said Dulles.[*]

The tasks of the theologian are to reflect critically on the Scriptures, using all the resources available, and to communicate what is found in an accessible and compelling way for the sake of the Christian faith and the Christian church. Presbyterian theologian Daniel Migliore describes the work of theology "as a continuing search for the fullness of the truth of God made known in Jesus Christ."[†]

Both the theologian as the specialist and the Christian believer who attends church and reads and studies the Scriptures can participate in the ongoing tasks of the theologian.

[*] Ibid., 10.
[†] Daniel L. Migliore, *Faith Seeking Understanding: An Introduction to Christian Theology*, 2nd ed. (Grand Rapids: Wm. B. Eerdmans Publishing Co., 2004), 1.

7. THE UNFINISHED TASKS OF THE THEOLOGIAN

As a theologian, one never runs out of work to do. The tasks of the theologian include listening to Scripture, studying Scripture, reflecting on the human condition, and then communicating what is heard and understood. Those tasks just keep on coming.

Whether it is the work of the theologian who is a specialist in theology or the work of theology done by a Christian believer in the context of a church, the ongoing tasks of the theologian keep one engaged fully and permanently. In other words, one never gets to the end of theology; there is always more to come.

This points to the nature of theology itself. Theology is not an attempt to once and for all say everything there is to say about God, the world, humanity, Christ, the future, and so forth. First of all, that would be impossible. Second, it would deny that there could be any more truth to break forth from God through God's Word!

Systematic theologians construct theological systems, or ways of expressing theological insights that are structured in organized, logical, and methodical ways. This is their task. One theologian said that the aim of dogmatics (i.e., theology) is "to attain intellectual clarity by ordering the given materials systematically."* Order and logic and method are indeed good things.

But we should never think that one particular presentation, expression, or system of theology says it all for all time. This is true both for creeds and confessions of faith as well as for theological systems or textbooks. Systems of theology and all

* Hendrikus Berkhof, *Introduction to the Study of Dogmatics* (Grand Rapids: Wm. B. Eerdmans Publishing Co., 1985), 10.

theological presentations should always be eminently revisable. They should be open to new insights and instruction from the Scriptures, as well as from the Holy Spirit.

There is always more work for theology to do. No one presentation of theology can say it all. As the great Baptist theologian Carlyle Marney used to say, "Theology never unpacks its bags and stays!"

Theologians recognize this about their theological formulations for several reasons. One is that our theological language can never completely capture all that God has said and done, as we learn of these things from the Scriptures. No single way of expressing God's truth can be exhaustive. There is always more to perceive, more to say. Our theological presentations are no substitutes for Scripture. Nor can they capture all the realities to which the Scriptures point.

A second reason why there are unfinished tasks of the theologian is theological. It is because all our theology can only, at best, point to but never capture the ultimate mystery with which theology deals: God. As Avery Dulles put it, "Systematization in theology can never be complete, for the true object of theology is the unfathomable mystery of God."[*] God as mystery can never be contained in human words.

So theologians construct their systems and write their books. This is good! But we do not absolutize our theological formulations and expressions. We know that as theologians, the best we can do is stammer. This led Hendrikus Berkhof to say that none of us writes our books "for all eternity; it is all 'wayfarers' theology' (*theologia viatorum*)."[†] We are always "on the way."

---

[*] Avery Dulles, *The Craft of Theology: From Symbol to System* (New York: Crossroad, 1992), 10.

[†] Berkhof, *Introduction to the Study of Dogmatics*, 38.

III. THEOLOGY FROM THE START

8. PARTS OF THEOLOGY: SLICING THE PIE

The field of theology has a number of parts—that is, there are different perspectives used to study the different aspects of theology. To break theology out into its parts means you have to "slice the pie." It's too big to consume as a whole; we need smaller, more manageable pieces.

Here are different parts of traditional theology:

- **Biblical theology.** The study of how the different ideas found in the Bible are understood in themselves and in relation to other biblical topics. Examples include covenant, salvation, life, and death. Biblical theology asks what the Bible teaches about these ideas.

- **Systematic theology.** The organized study of the main themes or doctrines of the Christian faith. Systematic theology tries to present a coherent understanding of what is found in the Scriptures using various tools such as philosophy, reason, and experience.

- **Historical theology.** The exploration of the historical contexts and situations in which theological ideas have developed since the beginning of the Christian era. Historical theology is the story of the church's attempt to formulate its faith and theologians' attempts to present the main themes of Christian theology in different historical periods and settings.

- **Philosophical theology.** The use of the tools of philosophy as an intellectual discipline to approach theological issues. Philosophical theology seeks to present Christian theology in terms that may seek a common point of contact with philosophers who study human knowledge and issues of truth.

- **Pastoral theology.** The study of the ways in which Christian theology has implications for the corporate and personal lives of those who are Christians. Pastoral theology stresses not only what one *knows* but also what one *feels* and the ways in which Christian beliefs affect the lives of Christian believers.

9. THE WEB OF THEOLOGY: THE OLD WOMAN IN THE SHOE

Studying theology means getting acquainted with a number of terms and ideas. As in all fields of study, theological ideas are interrelated. The study of theology leads from one idea to another. No matter where we start in our theological study, we will eventually get around to all the *loci* or "places" of theology. When we study the big ideas of theology, we find how they are interconnected. The more you learn about one aspect of theology, the more you are drawn into studying other aspects.

It's like that children's story of the old woman in the shoe. The dear old lady "had so many children, she didn't know what to do." Just imagine at night. When the children go to bed, Johnny calls her because he has to go to the bathroom. So she gets up and takes care of him. Beth has a bad dream, so she gets up to comfort her. Chrissy has a tummy ache, so the old woman gets up to give her some medicine. As soon as one child is taken care of, another has a need—so the old woman goes from one to another!

So it is in theology. When we learn about God, we are curious about how humans relate to God. When we study that, we ask, "Who is this Jesus Christ whom God sent into the world for humans?" And then we wonder, "What is the nature of this group of believers in Jesus Christ who join together to form a church?" When we study anthropology, we are led to study Christology, and then we are moved to exam ecclesiology. Like the old woman in the shoe, our study of one aspect of theology leads us into the study of others. All its interrelations make studying theology like being in a big web.

10. AUTHORITY IN THEOLOGY

One of the most basic questions in theology concerns authority. What counts as significant when one makes a theological statement? Is theology simply people sharing their opinions with others? Or are there some sources of authority to which we may appeal?

In the history of theology, three main sources of authority have been recognized. These three have played major roles in the great theological debates and in the theological statements that have been developed in response. They are Scripture, tradition, and inner revelation.

- **Scripture.** The Bible has been a major source of authority for theologians and for churches. It has been regarded as God's revelation. Thus, it is a source to which we should listen. Theologians have appealed to the Bible to justify their theological statements. The well-known evangelist Billy Graham was fond of proclaiming, "The Bible says!" So the Scriptures are basic sources for theological authority. In the sixteenth century, Martin Luther emphasized "Scripture alone" as the proper source of authority for the church, a perspective adopted widely within Protestantism.

- **Tradition.** The Bible has authority for the church, which, in turn, recognizes the Bible as an authority. The Roman Catholic Church and its theologians have argued that the early church existed before the Scriptures were canonized, or gathered together as the Bible. Since the church is the body that says the Scriptures are authoritative, then the church itself and its teachings, which interpret Scripture, should be regarded as authoritative too. Thus, the church itself and its teaching are also a source of authority for correct theology.

• **Inner revelation.** Some theologians and Christian believers have looked to one's individual experience of the Holy Spirit as the primary source of authority for their theology. A book (Scripture) or an institution (church) means nothing if the living Spirit of God does not illuminate a person and endow the person with the Holy Spirit. The Spirit dwelling in a person shows him or her what rightly to believe and what paths to follow in life. It is this inner revelation that is the direct means God uses to reveal God's self and to guide those who have received this illumination.

These three main sources of authority—Scripture, tradition, and inner revelation—are appealed to by theologians, but there is one more thing to say.

All the knowledge that comes to us from any and all these sources is interpreted by us. We use our reason as an eye, or lens or perspective, by which we evaluate what we believe the Bible is saying, or what the church is teaching, or what we believe the Holy Spirit is calling us toward. Reason is a complex system of dimensions in our lives and is influenced by many factors. But we are all interpreters of what we believe authoritative sources are saying. So reason plays a role in how we regard whatever elements of authority we appeal to whenever we make theological statements.

11. THEOLOGICAL TERMS: BACK TO BASICS

In the days when the New York Mets were having troubles in the National League and Yogi Berra was their manager, they had a particularly dismal game. Yogi was upset and closed off the clubhouse to reporters. He said to the players, "That game was terrible. It was the worst game I've ever seen. You guys should be ashamed of yourselves. We've got to go back to basics. This is a ball. This is a bat." Then from the corner of the clubhouse, the third-string catcher piped up and said, "Slow down, Yogi. You're going too fast!"

Theological terms are the basics for theology. We use language to articulate thoughts. Theological language, expressed in theological terms, is our way of expressing our thoughts about God, humanity, the church, and other theological realities. We use terms to construct ways of understanding these beliefs.

As in other disciplines, theology has a language to be recognized and learned. Theological terms have developed through the centuries in many languages in the discourse of theologians and in the church's life. To understand what theologians have to say and what the Christian church believes, it is important to become familiar with many of these terms.

Later in this book some definitions of key terms are given. There are also helpful theological dictionaries and handbooks listed in chap. 44, "A Brief List of Resources for Theological Study."

Theological terms are the building blocks that enable theological statements to be constructed. Let's go back to basics!

12. KEY THEOLOGICAL TERMS

Baptism

Initiation into the Christian faith through a worship ceremony in which water is applied by sprinkling, pouring, or immersion and done in the name of the Father, Son, and Holy Spirit (Trinitarian formula). It is regarded as a sacrament by most churches.

Christology

The study of the person and work of Jesus Christ. The church's understanding of who Jesus Christ is and what he has done grew and developed through the centuries. Early church councils produced christological statements.

Divine revelation

The self-disclosure and self-communication of God by which God conveys a knowledge of God to humans. It is important, since it makes known that which is inaccessible to human reason alone.

Doctrine

The Latin word *doctrina* means "teaching." Christian doctrine is what Christians understand the Scriptures to teach and the church to believe about theological topics or themes. Doctrines develop over time as new insights emerge and new ways of expression are used.

Ecclesiology

The study of the church as a biblical and theological topic. The New Testament presents various images of the church that the early church struggled with as it sought its self-understanding in light of the gospel and controversies.

Eschatology

The study of the last things or the end of the world. Theological dimensions include the second coming of Jesus Christ and the last judgment.

Incarnation

The doctrine that the eternal second Person of the Trinity assumed flesh and became a human being in Jesus of Nazareth. Jesus Christ was the "Word made flesh" (John 1:14). The doctrine holds that Jesus was one person with both a divine and a human nature.

Lord's Supper

The sacrament of Communion or the Eucharist. It celebrates the death of Christ, his presence with the church, and his future reign (kingdom). It was instituted by Jesus (1 Cor. 11:23–26) at the Last Supper, the final meal Jesus shared with his disciples before his crucifixion.

Sacraments

An outward sign instituted by God to convey an inward or spiritual grace. Sacraments are liturgical practices of churches. Roman Catholicism recognizes seven sacraments; Protestants recognize two—baptism and the Lord's Supper.

Salvation

God's activities in bringing humans into a right relationship with God and with one another through Jesus Christ. Humans are saved from the consequences of their sin and given eternal life. Biblical images for salvation vary widely.

Soteriology

The doctrine of salvation.

Theological anthropology

The doctrine of humanity, which views people in terms of their relationships to God. It includes critical reflection on issues such as the origin, purpose, and destiny of humankind in light of Christian theological understandings.

Trinity

The Christian church's belief that Father, Son, and Holy Spirit are three Persons in one Godhead. They share the same essence or substance (Gr. *homoousios*), yet they are three "persons" (Lat. *personae*).

IV. CHURCH THEOLOGY

13. THEOLOGY AND THE CHURCH

The work of doing theology can take place anytime, anywhere. It can take place by highly trained "professional" theologians or by Christian believers who study the Scriptures and seek to hear God's Word coming to them by the work of the Holy Spirit, wherever they are, whatever their situation may be.

For those who devote their lives to the study of theology and become theologians, or dogmaticians, different contexts for their work present themselves. As one theologian put it, "The dogmatician lives in two worlds, that of faith and that of scholarship."* Broadly speaking, there is the academic arena, which is marked by the work of theological scholarship over a wide range of topics. Academic theologians deal with theological issues of theoretical or practical interest and pursue the study of theology with a variety of approaches. The "academy" is a context in which the study of theology in its various forms can be carried out (see chap. 24, "Theology and the Academy").

The church is another setting in which the pursuit or study of theology is carried out. In the Christian context, the Christian church is the ongoing community that lives by its theological understandings and is in constant need of theological reflection as it seeks to live out its identity and mission in the world. Theology (or dogmatics) invites the church, as Karl Barth put it, "to listen again to the Word of God in the revelation to which Scripture testifies."† Theological work is in service to the Christian church in helping the church reflect

---

* Hendrikus Berkhof, *Introduction to the Study of Dogmatics* (Grand Rapids: Wm. B. Eerdmans Publishing Co., 1985), 14.

† Karl Barth, *Church Dogmatics*, I/2, ed. G. W. Bromiley and T. F. Torrance (Edinburgh: T. & T. Clark, 1963), 797.

upon, understand, and appropriate God's revelation. The church is both a hearing and a teaching church. It hears the Word of God and teaches it through preaching and instruction. All members of the church have this dual responsibility. Barth was clear that all the people of the church are to be involved actively in these tasks: "What a misuse it is of the idea of the congregation to understand by it a group of mere spectators privileged, or disqualified as such! The truth is that theologians cannot teach except as the mouthpiece of the congregation of Jesus Christ, which does not in any sense consist of listeners only, but of those who, as listeners, are themselves teachers."[*] The work of doing theology is for everyone in the church.

The study of theology and the work of doing theology carried out in church contexts orients the focus of theology to the Word of God—in Jesus Christ, in Scripture, in preaching. Barth's primary theological work was called *Church Dogmatics* because he believed theology in the church should be "a dogmatics of the ecumenical Church."[†] For him, church theology is the proper context for theological work, since "the Word of God did not found an academy but the Church."[‡]

As we study theology, we see it being carried out in a variety of settings. Some deal with purely academic questions of theological thought. Others are settings in which theology is done in the service of the church. In the church context, says Barth, theology seeks to "serve the reflection which the Church needs for its work, its struggle, its unavoidable temptations and sorrows." Theology serves "the Church of a specific time with its needs and hopes."[§]

[*] Ibid., 798.
[†] Ibid., 823.
[‡] Ibid., 841.
[§] Ibid.

14. THEOLOGY AND FAITH

In the midst of his classic work of Christian theology, *Institutes of the Christian Religion*, John Calvin (1509–1564) presented a definition of faith: "Faith is a firm and certain knowledge of God's benevolence toward us, founded upon the truth of the freely given promise in Christ, both revealed to our minds and sealed upon our hearts through the Holy Spirit."*

This definition unites faith and theology in these ways:

- Faith is tied to the "knowledge" of who God is and what God has done: "God's benevolence to us."
- Faith's content is theological in that faith is "founded upon the truth" of God's promise in Christ. Faith is not "empty"; it has substance to it.
- Faith is the promise of Christ "revealed to our minds" and "sealed upon our hearts." Faith is more than intellectual knowledge; it is a "personal knowledge" that is real to our "head" and our "heart."
- Faith comes to us by the Holy Spirit. Faith is the gift of God. It is not ours to achieve, but God's to give.

Theology can be defined as "faith asking questions." Theology for the Christian believer is the ongoing activity of faith seeking understanding. Christian theology in the church is not a neutral enterprise. It is the Christian vigorously seeking to experience more fully the knowledge of God and what God has done and is currently doing in this world. Theology carried out from the perspective of faith is the continuing work of learning and doing. And theology is about God!

* John Calvin, *Institutes of the Christian Religion*, ed. John T. McNeill (Philadelphia: Westminster Press, 1960), 3.2.7.

A wise theologian put it this way:

Christian faith is at bottom trust in and obedience to the free and gracious God made known in Jesus Christ. Christian theology is this same faith in the mode of asking questions and struggling to find at least provisional answers to these questions. Authentic faith is no sedative for world-weary souls, no satchel full of ready answers to the deepest questions of life. Instead, faith in God revealed in Jesus Christ sets an inquiry in motion, fights the inclination to accept things as they are, and continually calls in question unexamined assumptions about God, our world, and ourselves. Consequently, Christian faith has nothing in common with indifference to the search for truth, or fear of it, or the arrogant claim to possess it fully. True faith must be distinguished from fideism. Fideism says there comes a point where we must stop asking questions and must simply believe; faith keeps on seeking and asking. Theology grows out of this dynamism of Christian faith that incites reflection, inquiry, and pursuit of the truth not yet possessed, or only partially possessed.[*]

Christian theology emerges from faith and proceeds in faith. In faith we see that theology is always on its way.

[*] Daniel L. Migliore, *Faith Seeking Understanding: An Introduction to Christian Theology*, 2nd ed. (Grand Rapids: Wm. B. Eerdmans Publishing Co., 2004), 3.

15. FORMS OF CHRISTIANITY

After the death and resurrection of Jesus Christ, the early church spread throughout the Mediterranean world and beyond. Leaders in the church arose, variously called "bishops" and "elders." They worked within defined geographical areas. The bishop of Rome became the most prominent church leader. This marked the beginning of the papacy and what became known as the Roman Catholic Church. There are now three major forms or divisions of Christianity.

- **Roman Catholicism.** The primacy of the bishop of Rome developed because Rome was the leading city of the early Christian era. This was reinforced by the interpretation of Matthew 16:18, in which Jesus says to Peter, "And I tell you, you are Peter [Gr. *petros*], and on this rock [Gr. *petra*] I will build my church, and the gates of Hades will not prevail against it." The growing powers of the bishop of Rome were expressed in numerous theological statements, and during the early Middle Ages (600–1050), the "vicar of St. Peter" was recognized as the central focus of Western Christendom. The Roman Catholic Church, structured hierarchically with the pope as the "vicar of Christ" at its head, was the sole ecclesiastical expression of Christianity.

- **Eastern Orthodoxy.** Orthodox churches today developed from the church of the Byzantine Empire, so the primary influences upon them have been Greek. A series of theological controversies in early Christianity resulted in some churches in the East being sympathetic to viewpoints that did not become predominant in the West. The churches of Rome and Constantinople became more estranged from each other, leading to a lasting division. The final break came in AD 1054, when disputes arose over the claims of the pope and the theological question of whether the Holy Spirit proceeds from the Father, or from the Father and the Son (Lat. *filioque*; "and the Son"). Today the leading figure of Orthodox churches is the patriarch of Constantinople.

- **Protestantism.** Reaction against the theology and practices of the medieval Roman Catholic Church was led by the German monk Martin Luther (1483–1546). Luther objected to church teachings and actions he believed were not in accord with the teachings of Scripture, particularly the New Testament. In 1517, he issued his Ninety-five Theses, a list of detailed complaints. His further writings led to his excommunication by the pope. Luther and his followers and sympathizers established Protestantism. This movement has broken into a number of "denominations" of Protestants, with the historic divisions being Lutheran, Reformed, Anglican, and Anabaptist. All rejected Roman Catholic theology, but each has its own distinct theological viewpoints.

16. DENOMINATIONS

In some small towns, there seems to be a church on every corner. Some big cities boast a variety of church buildings, ranging from Gothic cathedrals to storefronts. Each usually has a sign that identifies the church by its name and frequently its denomination.

"Denomination" comes from the Latin term *denominare* ("to name"). It is our way of identifying things such as money or churches. One Internet database gives information on 9,000 Christian denominations.[*] Some say there are around 38,000 Christian denominations![†]

Most of these denominations began out of theological convictions. The major splits in Christianity itself—in 1054 when the Eastern church and the Western church separated and in the sixteenth century when the Protestant Reformation led to a number of different theological movements—were caused largely by differences in theology (see chart).

Each of the Christian denominations today has certain theological beliefs about the main elements of Christianity. If these denominations align themselves with historic Christianity at all, they will have views about the Bible, God, Jesus Christ, the church, sacraments, and so forth. They will also look to various sources of authority, such as Scripture, tradition, and inner revelation, from which to draw their theologies and to construct any positive statement of what they believe. There are different ways to analyze denominations: historically, culturally, sociologically. But the different denominations maintain distinctive viewpoints that have emerged specifically from their theological understandings of Christian faith.

[*] World Christian Database, Center for the Study of Global Christianity, Gordon-Conwell Theological Seminary, http://worldchristiandatabase.org/wcd.

[†] Christianity Today, General Statistics and Facts of Christianity, http://christianity.about.com/od/denominations/p/christiantoday.htm.

Major Branches and Movements of Protestantism

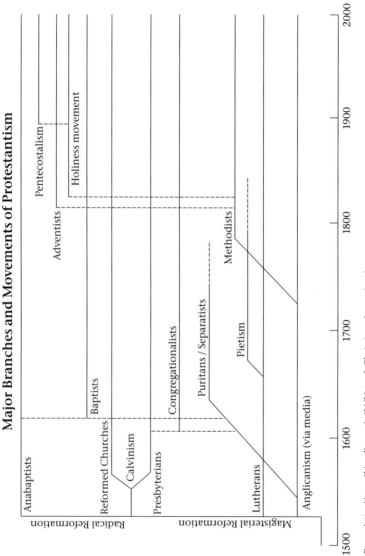

From: http://en.wikipedia.org/wiki/List_of_Christian_denominations

17. MAJOR BELIEFS OF DENOMINATIONS

Seventh-Day Adventist Churches

Authority—Bible and religious experience
Bible—Revelation of God without error
Salvation—Jesus is the savior who offers God's love for acceptance
Church—Believers in Christ who will remain faithful in latter days
Church government—Representative collective bodies
Sacraments—Believer's baptism by immersion; Lord's Supper is memorial meal

Anabaptist Churches

Authority—Scripture along with religious experience
Bible—God's revelation understood only through life of discipleship
Salvation—By faith in Jesus Christ leading to a life of obedience
Church—Community of believers who are faithful disciples of Christ
Church government—Congregational
Sacraments—Believer's baptism only; Lord's Supper a memorial meal

Anglican/Episcopal Churches

Authority—Scripture, church tradition, and reason
Bible—The revelation of God to be interpreted by reason and tradition

Salvation—By faith in Jesus Christ as presented by the church

Church—The body of Christian believers

Church government—Hierarchical through apostolic succession back to the days of the apostles

Sacraments—Baptism and the Lord's Supper are central to church life

Baptist Churches

Authority—Bible alone

Bible—God's Word, usually considered inerrant in all it affirms

Salvation—By faith in Jesus Christ, with emphasis on human decision

Church—Those who are redeemed in Christ, focused in local congregations

Church government—Congregational

Sacraments—Baptism is an ordinance and must be by immersion; Lord's Supper is a memorial

Christian Churches (Disciples of Christ)

Authority—Bible and religious experience

Bible—Revelation of God pointing to Jesus Christ

Salvation—By faith, repentance, and baptism

Church—Body of Christian believers

Church government—Congregational

Sacraments—Believer's baptism by immersion; Lord's Supper is a memorial

Congregational Churches

Authority—The Bible as God's revelation; confessions interpret Scripture

Bible—Revelation of God interpreted by individuals
Salvation—By God's grace through faith in Jesus Christ
Church—Body of Christ's disciples
Church government—Congregational
Sacraments—Infant or believer's baptism; Lord's Supper

Holiness and Pentecostal Churches

Authority—The Bible and the experience of the Holy Spirit
Bible—God's Word without error
Salvation—By faith to be born again; proved by a life of holiness
Church—Those who have received the baptism of the Holy Spirit
Church government—Congregational
Sacraments—Baptism by immersion; second baptism by Holy Spirit gives spiritual gifts; Lord's Supper is a memorial

Lutheran Churches

Authority—Scripture alone is acknowledged
Bible—Revelation of God to be interpreted by individuals
Salvation—By God's grace through faith
Church—The community of people who believe in Jesus Christ
Church government—Hierarchical; bishops are elected leaders of judicatories
Sacraments—Baptism and Lord's Supper

Methodist Churches

Authority—Scripture, tradition, reason, personal religious experience
Bible—God's revelation

Salvation—By faith alone; emphasize human "free will" in salvation

Church—The body of Christ

Church government—Hierarchical, with bishops and district superintendents as central

Sacraments—Baptism and Lord's Supper

Orthodox Churches

Authority—Scripture and apostolic tradition through patriarchs

Bible—Source of revelation, along with church tradition

Salvation—Through deification of believers to be united more fully with God

Church—The body of Christ

Church government—Patriarch of Constantinople is visible head; other patriarchs govern

Sacraments—Recognize seven *mysteries* (baptism, chrismation, Communion, confession, marriage, holy orders, and anointing of the sick), but formal number is not limited

Reformed and Presbyterian Churches

Authority—Scripture is the source of authority; confessions interpret Scripture

Bible—God's revelation, with various views about the nature of Scripture

Salvation—By God's grace through the gift of faith given by the Holy Spirit, emphasizing God's election and initiative in salvation

Church—The "elect" of God, or those who acknowledge Jesus Christ as Lord and Savior

Church government—Presbyterian or congregational system

Sacraments—Baptism and Lord's Supper

Roman Catholic Churches

Authority—Pope and church tradition's interpretation of Scripture becomes authoritative

Bible—Revelation of God but rightly interpreted by the church

Salvation—Through faith, which is believing what the church teaches

Church—The divine institution, which is the means of salvation

Church government—Pope (vicar of Christ) and the Magisterium, the hierarchy of cardinals, archbishops, and bishops

Sacraments—Seven, from cradle to grave (baptism, Eucharist, reconciliation, confirmation, marriage, holy orders, anointing of the sick)

18. THEOLOGY IN CREEDS, CONFESSIONS, AND CATECHISMS

Theology is a "second order" work. That is, traditional theology is a human articulation of realities derived from Scripture. Theology is not identical with Scripture. It is a way of trying to say what the Scriptures mean about different themes or topics.

Theology is written by theologians. It is also of primary concern for the Christian churches. Churches often use *creeds* or *confessions of faith* to articulate their beliefs about the important teachings of Scripture that are in the form of Christian doctrines.

"Creed" comes from the Latin word *credo*, meaning "I believe." A creed is a statement of faith, a way of saying what a faith community understands about the Christian faith. The psalmist declared, "Let the redeemed of the Lord say so" (Ps. 107:2). In the Old Testament, the nation of Israel confessed its faith in its Lord in the Shema: "Hear, O Israel: The Lord is our God, the Lord alone" (Deut. 6:4).

In the New Testament, Jesus gave his disciples a "midterm examination" in the midst of his ministry and asked them, "Who do people say that the Son of Man is?" Peter answered with a confession of faith: "You are the Messiah, the Son of the living God" (Matt. 16:13–16).

Brief summary statements about the meaning and importance of the life, death, and resurrection of Jesus Christ were offered by Paul (1 Cor. 15:3–4; Rom. 1:3–4). Perhaps the oldest Christian creed is "Jesus Christ is Lord," found in the "Christ hymn" of Philippians 2:5–11.

The Christian community affirmed its faith in a body of belief that in the period of the early church became more formal and structured. Later, creeds came to be called "confessions" as they became more detailed. Some later confessions gave a panoramic view of Christian doctrine, while other statements by church bodies were focused on particular situations, issues, or beliefs. Confessions of faith frequently say both positively what is believed and negatively what beliefs are to be rejected.

Creeds and confessions function as ways to pass along the Christian tradition.* They seek to provide a measure of unity among varieties of churches and to establish a measure of identity—so Christian people know who they are and what they believe. Creeds are spoken or sung in worship as a means of praising God—as statements about what God has said and done. They can provide resources for teaching and preaching as the church articulates its understandings of its shared Christian belief. Creeds also can serve as guides for interpreting Scripture, since creedal expressions indicate ways in which the church has read the Bible through the centuries. They can clarify what is *orthodoxy*, or right belief, according to the church, and what is *heresy*, or what is wrong and dangerous for belief.

Important Creeds, Confessions, and Catechisms

Early Church

Nicene Creed, AD 325; Constantinople, AD 381
Athanasian Creed, c. AD 500
Apostles' Creed, 2nd–9th centuries

* A helpful collection of documents can be found at http://64.33.81.65/index.htm.

Sixteenth-Century Reformation

Schleitheim Articles, 1527 (Anabaptist)
Martin Luther's Small Catechism, 1529 (Lutheran)
Martin Luther's Large Catechism, 1530 (Lutheran)
Augsburg Confession, 1530 (Lutheran)
French Confession, 1559 (Reformed)
Scots Confession, 1560 (Reformed)
Belgic Confession, 1561 (Reformed)
Decrees of the Council of Trent, 1563 (Roman Catholic)
Heidelberg Catechism, 1563 (Reformed)
Second Helvetic Confession, 1566 (Reformed)
Thirty-nine Articles, 1571 (Anglican)
Formula of Concord, 1577 (Lutheran)
Dordrecht Confession, 1632 (Anabaptist)
Westminster Confessions and Catechisms, 1647 (Reformed)
London Baptist Confessions, 1664, 1689 (Baptist)
Confession of Dositheus, 1672 (Orthodox)

Modern Era

Articles of Religion, 1784 (Methodist)
New Hampshire Confession, 1832 (Baptist)
Baltimore Catechism, 1891 (Roman Catholic)
Barmen Declaration, 1934 (Confessing Church, Germany)
Dogmatic Constitution on the Church, 1964 (Roman Catholic, Vatican Council II)
Confession of 1967 (Reformed)
Our Song of Hope, 1978 (Reformed)
Belhar Confession, 1986 (Reformed, South Africa)
Brief Statement of Faith, 1991 (Reformed)

Ecumenical Statements

The Call to Unity, 1927 (Lausanne)

The Grace of Our Lord Jesus Christ, 1937 (Edinburgh)

The Relation of the Church to the War in Light of Christian Faith, 1943 (Federal Council of Churches)

Message of the First Assembly of the World Council of Churches, 1948 (Amsterdam)

The Church's Unity, 1961 (World Council of Churches, New Delhi)

The Kairos Document, 1985 (South Africa)

19. THEOLOGY AND THE BIBLE

There are different ways of approaching theology and carrying out the work of theology. Through the centuries, Christians have used a variety of methods to do theological reflection. Common to them all is some place for the Bible as a source or norm for authority.

The Christian tradition has asserted that the Bible is God's revelation of who God is and what God has done. This has been understood in a host of different ways. As I have written elsewhere, the various theologies we encounter have "their own ways of understanding the nature of Scripture and its appropriate interpretation. What a Christian theology says about the Bible will significantly affect its concerns and the rest of its approach in general."*

In Christian churches, the Bible holds a central place. Protestantism in particular has stressed the centrality of Scripture as God's Word that comes to us in Jesus Christ who is the "Word of God" (John 1:1), in the Scriptures, and in preaching. As one church confession puts it, in Holy Scripture, "the universal Church of Christ has the most complete exposition of all that pertains to a saving faith, and also to the framing of a life acceptable to God."† The purpose of Scripture is theological in that it relates to salvation. It is also ethical or practical in

* Donald K. McKim, *The Bible in Theology and Preaching* (repr., Eugene, OR: Wipf & Stock, 1999), 15; see further for a survey of contemporary viewpoints about the nature and function of the Bible. A complement to this work is McKim, ed., *A Guide to Contemporary Hermeneutics: Major Trends in Biblical Interpretation* (repr., Eugene, OR: Wipf & Stock, 1999). Also helpful is Justin S. Holcomb, ed., *Christian Theologies of Scripture: A Comparative Introduction* (New York: New York University Press, 2006).

† The Second Helvetic Confession (1566), a Reformed confession written by Heinrich Bullinger. See *Book of Confessions: Study Edition*, Office of the General Assembly, Presbyterian Church (U.S.A.) (Louisville, KY: Geneva Press, 1996), 5.002.

that it points the way to the kind of life God wants the people of God to live.

So theology in the church is inextricably connected to the Bible. The Bible becomes the source from which theological reflection and understanding begins.

One theologian has put it this way:

> The final norm is Jesus Christ, the living Word of God, who is attested in Holy Scripture and proclaimed by the church through the ages. Both the Bible and church proclamation become transparent to this living Word when they are illumined by the Spirit for the community of the faithful. When confronted by the illuminated text, we are at the same time meeting the risen Christ. Through the agency of the Spirit the understanding of the text becomes a redemptive happening, a break-through into meaning.[*]

Recognizing the Bible's authority and place in theology does not answer all the questions—not by a long shot! More questions throng—about the nature of Scripture, its appropriate interpretation, the role of the Holy Spirit in biblical interpretation, ways in which we understand biblical meanings in contemporary contexts, and many more. Theologians will always be engaged with the Bible!

As we study theology, we recognize the central role played by the Bible, both historically and for today. Some theologians cite more biblical passages and do more biblical interpretation than others. But theology that is oriented toward the church community will find itself grounded in Scripture. As a contemporary Presbyterian confession put it:

---

[*] Donald G. Bloesch, *Holy Scripture: Revelation, Inspiration, and Interpretation*, Christian Foundations (Downers Grove, IL: InterVarsity Press, 1994), 159.

The one sufficient revelation of God is Jesus Christ, the Word of God incarnate, to whom the Holy Spirit bears unique and authoritative witness through the Holy Scriptures, which are received and obeyed as the word of God written. The church has received the books of the Old and New Testaments as prophetic and apostolic testimony in which it hears the word of God and by which its faith and obedience are nourished and regulated.[*]

---

[*] The Confession of 1967, in *Book of Confessions,* 9.27.

20. THEOLOGY AND THE CHRISTIAN YEAR

Christian churches mark time by the liturgical year. The different days, seasons, and festivals provide a rhythm and bring a focus to the actions of God, giving meaning and significance to the flow of days. The liturgical year orients us to remember and relive God's ongoing actions in history.

The liturgical year features major seasons in which there are important theological emphases. Theology helps shape Christian understandings of the meaning of significant days and seasons.

Major days and seasons of the liturgical year include:

- **Advent** (Lat. *adventus*; "coming") is the season of anticipation of the coming of Christ. Christ's first coming was his incarnation; his second coming will be his future coming in glory. Advent is the four Sundays before Christmas. Theologically the season focuses on God's promises to send a messiah; in terms of Christ's second Advent, the season focuses on the ultimate triumph and reign of God in Jesus Christ.

- **Christmas** (Old Eng. *Christus mass*) is the festival day and season marking the birth of Jesus Christ, celebrated on December 25. The church's belief that Jesus Christ is the eternal Son of God who came to earth to live and die and be raised again to bring salvation is celebrated as the incarnation of Jesus Christ. The fullness of Jesus' life and work is celebrated for twelve days from December 25 until January 5.

- **Epiphany** (Gr. *epiphaneia*; "manifestation") is the church festival celebrated on January 6 to commemorate the visit of the Magi to the Christ child (Matt. 2:1–12).

Theologically, Epiphany marks the manifestation of the Messiah to the Gentiles and thus to the whole world. This marks the widening of the Messiah's mission to the whole world, and in the recognition by the Magi, the world as a whole is to recognize the person of Jesus Christ as the supreme Lord of all. Following Epiphany Sunday, the church marks Jesus' baptism, in which Jesus identifies with humanity and submits himself to the will of God. Transfiguration Sunday, which is celebrated in some Christian denominations during the season of Epiphany, marks Jesus' appearance in a form of glory as he appeared on a mountaintop with Elijah and Moses (Matt. 17:1–13 and parallels). This incident previewed his resurrection and the light and glory that will characterize the ultimate reign of Christ.

- **Lent** (Middle Eng. *lente*; "spring"; Old Eng. *lengthen*; "to lengthen [daylight]") is the forty-day period prior to Easter. It begins with Ash Wednesday, which is a day of penitence and repentance. Sin is remembered, recognized, and renounced. The Lenten season is a period of prolonged reflection on one's life, marked often by spiritual disciplines in which one's relationship with God is examined. Theologically, it marks an expression of the desire to turn from the vestiges of sin in one's life and to renew one's sense of devotion to following Jesus Christ as Lord and Savior.

- **Holy Week.** The three days that complete the week before Easter commemorate the final events in Jesus' life. Maundy Thursday (Lat. *mandatum*; "mandate, commandment") marks Jesus' command to his disciples to show love by following his example, displayed in the washing of the disciples' feet (John 13:5–17). Jesus' "new commandment" of love is to be a mark of discipleship (John 13:34). Good Friday is the holy day on which the death of Jesus on the cross is remembered. Although the putting to death of the innocent Son of God was the most heinous crime in history, the church has called this day "Good" Friday in recognition that it is through Jesus' crucifixion that salvation is given for the world. Through his death, sin is forgiven, guilt is gone, and new life in a loving relationship with God is made possible. The cross is the central symbol of Christianity to recognize the importance of Jesus' death as the means for God and sinners to be reconciled and the liberation of humanity to be enacted. Holy Saturday is a day of silence in which Jesus' lying in the tomb is remembered. This is a day of somber reverence in which the events of Jesus' life and the power of his death are recognized.

- **Easter** is the Sunday following Good Friday and the subsequent season, which lasts for fifty days (including Sundays) until Pentecost. The day and the season celebrate the resurrection of Jesus Christ from the dead. It is a time of glorious rejoicing in the victory of Christ over the powers of sin and evil. It establishes Christian hope for the ultimate triumph of God's reign in Christ and the hope of resurrection for all who are in Christ, who is "the first fruits of those who have died" (1 Cor. 15:20).

- **Ascension Day** remembers the ascension of Jesus to heaven (Acts 1:3–11), celebrated forty days after Easter Sunday. Theologically, it recognizes that Jesus is "at the right hand of God" (Rom. 8:34) and now carries out ministries of intercession on behalf of Christian believers. This is marked as well by the image of Jesus as the "great high priest" (Heb. 4:14) who now sympathizes with our weaknesses and gives believers confidence to "approach the throne of grace with boldness" (Heb. 4:16).

- **Pentecost** (Gr. *pentēkostē*; "fiftieth"). With roots in the Jewish festival of Weeks (Exod. 23:14–17) when the firstfruits of the harvest were offered to God, fifty days after

Passover, Pentecost is now celebrated as both a day and a season. Fifty days after the resurrection of Jesus Christ, the Holy Spirit was poured out upon the early Christian believers (Acts 2). Theologically, this joyful celebration recognizes God's presence with Christian believers in giving the gift of the Holy Spirit to lead and guide the church and to sustain and nourish the lives of Christian believers by the indwelling of the Spirit (Rom. 8:11). Reflection on the nature of the church and the process of sanctification (growth in holiness) in the Christian life are appropriate theological focuses in the Pentecost season. This is the longest season of the church year and is sometimes called "Ordinary Time."

- **Christ the King.** The "last Sunday" of the Christian year is the celebration of the reign of Jesus Christ (Col. 1:11–20; Rev. 1:4b–8). Theologically, this Sunday anticipates the fullness of the reign of God in Jesus Christ and the consummation of human history. It recognizes the present lordship of Christ, established in the life, death, and resurrection of Jesus Christ, as the one whose reign is taking shape in the world today. The final fulfillment of the reign of Christ is anticipated in the Lord's Prayer with the petition "Your kingdom come" (Matt. 6:10).

21. THEOLOGY AND PREACHING

From its earliest days, the Christian church has lived by preaching. Paul wrote to the Romans that "faith comes from what is heard and what is heard comes through the word of Christ" (Rom. 10:17). Preaching is the primary means by which the gospel of Jesus Christ is communicated and the means by which faith is born.

Preaching proclaims Christ, and in that way Jesus Christ becomes real and present through the preaching event. The church's theology of preaching has recognized that "it takes three to preach." There is the preacher who proclaims, the congregation that hears, and the Holy Spirit by whose work preaching becomes effective in human lives. As John Calvin put it, "The foundation of faith would be frail and unsteady if it rested on human wisdom; and therefore, as preaching is the instrument of faith, so the Holy Spirit makes preaching efficacious."*

When preaching is effective in this way, the word of God has been proclaimed and heard and received in faith. The Second Helvetic Confession, a Reformed confession written by Heinrich Bullinger (1504–1575) in 1566, proclaimed that "the preaching of the Word of God is the Word of God."

Theological understandings, therefore, undergird the church's views of preaching. Even if some would not express the exact formulation from Bullinger, Christian faith does recognize that preaching is a means by which God's actions in Jesus Christ are proclaimed. Karl Barth wrote, "Preaching aims

* John Calvin, "Commentary on Ephesians 1:13," in *Galatians, Ephesians, Philippians and Colossians*, trans. T. H. L. Parker, Calvin's New Testament Commentaries, ed. David W. Torrance and Thomas F. Torrance (repr., Grand Rapids: Wm. B. Eerdmans Publishing Co., 1980), 131.

at the people of a specific time to tell them that their lives have their basis and hope in Jesus Christ."[*]

This conviction also led Barth to reflect on the relationship between theology ("dogmatics" in Barth's terms) and preaching. Christian preaching should be grounded in the church's best theological understanding of the gospel of Christ. Barth went so far as to say that "proclamation is essential, dogmatics is needed only for the sake of it."[†]

The work of preachers who preach and the work of theologians who do theology are both essential for the church. They are integrally related to each other. One more image from Barth: "Dogmatics and preaching are related in the same way as service at headquarters and at the front. Headquarters has to be there if anything essential is to be done at the front. Dogmatics has to serve the church. It has to help to purify doctrine."[‡]

The theologian serves the church as does the preacher. Both serve to proclaim Jesus Christ.

[*] Karl Barth, *Homiletics* (Louisville, KY: Westminster/John Knox Press, 1991), 89.

[†] Karl Barth, *Church Dogmatics*, I/1, ed. G. W. Bromiley and T. F. Torrance, 2nd ed. (repr., Edinburgh: T. & T. Clark, 1980), 87.

[‡] Karl Barth, *The Göttingen Dogmatics*, ed. Hannelotte Reiffen (Grand Rapids: Wm. B. Eerdmans Publishing Co., 1991), 276.

22. THEOLOGY AND PRAYER

It is easy to "do theology" by becoming immersed in all kinds of intellectual exercises, arguments, and interpretations in order to "make your point." These are the elements that often go into formal theology. In this regard, theology—like other endeavors—is an intellectual exercise. But the great theologians of the church have recognized something more is needed, and it is needed at the very beginning of the theological enterprise. This ingredient is prayer.

Theology begins in prayer and with prayer. The theologian commends all the theologizing to be done to the mercy and grace of God, asking that God will use this theological work for God's purposes and the service of God in the world. Ultimately, theology—as all else—should be done for the glory of God (1 Cor. 10:31). Theology as the study of God has a purpose: to understand God and to make God known. This is what the prayer that begins our theological work is intended to seek.

In 1078 the great medieval theologian Anselm wrote a book, *Proslogion*, which means "Discourse," in which he presented an argument to establish the existence of God. This is sometimes called the "ontological argument." But the whole argument of the book is cast in the form of a prayer. It is a deep meditation on Christian faith and is an example of Anselm's theological method of "faith seeking understanding."

At the beginning, the theologian invokes God: "Come then, Lord my God, teach my heart where and how to seek You, and where and how to find You."* Then follows his sustained argument for the existence of God as "something than which nothing greater can be thought."

* Anselm of Canterbury, *Proslogion*, in Anselm, *The Major Works*, ed. Brian Davies and G. R. Evans (New York: Oxford University Press, 1998), 84–85.

The establishment of this argument brings Anselm great joy. At the end he writes, "I pray, O God, that I may know You and love You, so that I may rejoice in You."[*]

In the tradition of Anselm, Karl Barth said, "The first and basic act of theological work is *prayer*. . . . Without prayer there can be no theological work."[†] Prayer is no substitute for thinking hard and studying hard in doing theology. As Barth said, "Where theology is concerned, the rule *Ora et labora*! is valid under all circumstances—pray and work."[‡]

The work of theology is work. As one does theological reflection, there are no shortcuts to considering thoughts and ideas, to writing, and to speaking about what one finds. As Barth put it, "Theological work can be done only in the indissoluble unity of prayer and study. Prayer without study would be empty. Study without prayer would be blind."[§] Good theology begins in prayer. It is a work of devotion, of service to God in Christ, for the sake of the church.

Anselm concluded his *Proslogion* with the words of this prayer to the God of truth: "Let my heart meditate on it, let my tongue speak of it, let my heart love it, let my mouth preach it. Let my soul hunger for it, let my flesh thirst for it, my whole being desire it, until I enter into the 'joy of the Lord' [Matt. 25:21], who is God, Three in One, 'blessed forever. Amen' [Rom. 1:25]."[¶]

[*] Ibid., 103.
[†] Karl Barth, *Evangelical Theology* (London: Collins, 1969), 149.
[‡] Ibid.
[§] Ibid., 159.
[¶] Anselm, *Proslogion*, 104.

23. THEOLOGY AND SERVICE

The apostle Paul told the Corinthian Christians, "For we do not proclaim ourselves; we proclaim Jesus Christ as Lord" (2 Cor. 4:5). Central to the Christian gospel is the proclamation of Jesus Christ, and not of human personalities or gains or "success."

Christian theology does not exist for itself or to gain praise as being brilliantly articulated or scrupulously argued. Christian theology points beyond itself to its content: the being and actions of the living God. Theology is not an end in itself. It is an "open window" into the activities of God in the past, present, and future. Theology offers itself, in whatever forms it takes, to the greater service of the glory of God and to the glory of God as found in the person and work of the Lord Jesus Christ.

The same is true of the theologian who does theology. We do not do theological reflection and articulate our perspectives for our own sakes. We do not seek glamour and praise for being acute thinkers or brilliant theologians. To do so would be to do what the apostle did not want: proclaim ourselves.

Instead, the theologian provides theological thought in the service of the church, as a service. It is a vocation, or calling: to do the work of a theologian for the sake of the church's life and thought. Theological activities are not done to garner the praise of others or to enhance one's stature. They are done for the purposes of the church's mission and its own service in the world.

Karl Barth said theology is to be "a modest undertaking which like missionary work can only aim to serve rather than to dominate by rendering a certain limited and transitory assistance to the cause of the community and therefore of all Christians and the world as a whole."* Theology is in service to the church and to the world.

---

* Karl Barth, *Church Dogmatics*, IV/3, ed. G. W. Bromiley and T. F. Torrance (repr., Edinburgh: T. & T. Clark, 1992), 881.

Barth said also that "every act of theological work must have the character of an offering in which everything is placed before the living God."[*] Doing theology, serving as a theologian, is an act of devotion to the living God who has come among us in Jesus Christ, whom we proclaim. We give our whole selves to the theological task, just as God in Christ has given us the message of the gospel.

---

[*] Karl Barth, *Evangelical Theology* (London: Collins, 1969), 155.

V. THEOLOGY
AND . . .

24. THEOLOGY AND THE ACADEMY

The study of theology is carried on in the church and also as an academic discipline. One can earn an advanced academic degree in the study of theology from a university or from a theological seminary. Those who teach theology in academic settings have academic credentials that say they have made a formal study of theology as a field of inquiry or a body of knowledge.

Sometimes this is called the "scientific" study of theology. Like those who study other topics in an academic manner, the "scientific theologian" approaches the study of theology as an astronomer studies the stars, a zoologist studies animal life, or a lawyer studies the law. As one theologian put it, "scientific approach" is "a striking way of putting it because it indicates that a person first takes some distance from the field of study, the distance of dispassionate observation, which a person then tries to bridge by a process of reflection. So the scholar lives between experience and reflection."*

"Academy" is a term sometimes used to describe this "scientific approach" to the study of a topic, including theology. Those who have formal education and degrees, who teach and write about theology, become recognized by peers and others as theologians. In the United States, those who are scholars and teach religion—including theology—often belong to the American Academy of Religion, an organization that brings together scholars for study and discussion. In this venue, one can approach the study of religion in general, with Christian theology being just one small section. In these contexts, a theologian works on the basis of established academic

* Hendrikus Berkhof, *Introduction to the Study of Dogmatics* (Grand Rapids: Wm. B. Eerdmans Publishing Co., 1985), 14.

procedures and may or may not be a person who professes a personal Christian faith. Here, the theologian's particular religious experience is not necessarily regarded as a significant factor in whether what intellectual results are produced will be regarded as significant. Theologians who work in university settings may find themselves operating primarily in this type of academic mode. Theologians who teach in seminaries also adopt a scientific approach to the study of theology, but they are more likely to explore other dimensions to theology that coincide more directly with questions and issues that are important for the Christian theological tradition and contemporary Christian churches.

The issues and questions dealt with by theologians in the academy may or may not overlap the concerns of theology, which is focused on the church and on faith. The emphasis in the academy is on academic scholarship and the study of theology as an intellectual discipline. In this regard, theology relates to a number of other academic areas. Among the most important are:

- philosophy, since many philosophical assumptions and questions directly relate to theology;

- the Bible, since the Hebrew and Christian Scriptures are so central to the study of theology, both as a church subject and an academic subject;

- culture, since all theology and theological statements are carried out in a particular social and cultural context; and

- science, since both theology and science make statements about "reality" from their own perspectives.

25. THEOLOGY AND PHILOSOPHY

Someone explained the difference between a philosopher and theologian this way: A philosopher is like a person in a dark room looking for a black cat, which isn't there. A theologian is like a person in a dark room looking for a black cat, which isn't there—and who finds it!

Philosophy means "love of wisdom." For centuries humans have been thinking about the important issues of life: What is reality? How do we know anything? Who am I? Is there any power beyond humans? Philosophers have used a variety of means to discuss these questions and to come to a variety of conclusions, the primary one being the power of reason. One can begin with certain assumptions and then by various means, including reason, come to conclusions.

Theology means "study of God." Theology also deals with important issues of life. A difference with philosophy is that theology includes belief in the existence of God. In the Christian tradition of theology, this God is known through God's revelation—especially in the Bible. Thus, our perspectives on life and its big questions have a source of input or authority that philosophy does not necessarily acknowledge—the God who is revealed in Scripture. Biblical perspectives play a role in theology, while philosophy proceeds on the basis of human reason or perceptions.

26. THEOLOGY AND CULTURE

All theological statements or systems of theology are constructed by people who live and breathe and work in specific times and places and cultures. That should seem self-evident. Yet in the past, these dimensions have often not been recognized. Many theologians have assumed that what they were doing was "timeless" and "cultureless," that they were constructing theological formulations that transcended the shaping forces that come into play when we try to say something about God or Jesus Christ or the church or any topic in theology.

Yet theology always comes out of specific cultural contexts. Culture (Lat. *colere*; "to till, to cultivate") in the broadest sense refers to all human activities and endeavors. It is the comprehensive blanket in which we are wrapped as humans. The intellectual, social, and personal milieus of our lives help shape who we are, how we think and act, and how we articulate our understandings. These and other factors affect our theological statements.

So, inherently, theology has limits. Its limits reflect human limitations themselves. Our limits reflect the cultures in which we live and the values we imbibe from them. Our training and education, the intellectual sources we know, the way we view the nature and function of theology itself—all these and more—affect us. This means no one can construct a complete theological system that addresses in a timeless manner all there is to know and say about God, God's relation to the world, and all the questions that theology wrestles with in an ongoing way.

Justo L. González and Zaida Maldonado Pérez put it like this:

The way in which theology most frequently ignores its limits is by forgetting that it always exists within a context, and that from that context it derives a perspective that is always partial, concrete, and provisional. Too often theologians have imagined that what they say does not reflect their own circumstances, and that therefore it is God's own truth. When someone then sees or interprets a particular point of theology from a different perspective, that person seems to be questioning, not what those theologians have said, but God's revelation. But the truth is that every theology has its own perspective, its own historical setting, which lead it to ask certain questions, and that therefore no theology is universal or perennial, that is, equally valid in all places or for all times.[*]

This does not mean that anything goes in theology or that everything is up for grabs—that there are no ways to evaluate different theological claims or that anything said can be passed off as a valid theological statement. Of course not!

Traditionally, theology has to begin with God and God's revelation, what we know of God. For most theologians, this revelation is centered in the Scriptures of the Old and New Testament and in Jesus Christ, who is presented to us there. Theology proceeds by testing its statements in relation to this revelation. So not every statement to be made can be said to be an appropriate interpretation of God's revelation. Not all theological statements are good or true.

Recognizing the contextual and cultural dimensions of theology is simply to indicate an awareness that all our theologies and theological statements are incomplete or partial, that they reflect the realities of the lives of those making the statements, and that they are statements of perspectives that are shaped by human, cultural dimensions.

[*] Justo L. González and Zaida Maldonado Pérez, *An Introduction to Christian Theology* (Nashville: Abingdon Press, 2002), 29–30.

Yet this is actually good news! It widens our scope and opens our ears to voices beyond our own and to approaches outside our own, limited selves. We can be open and appreciative of ways of expression and formulations that come from others in their cultural contexts. This can enhance and deepen our own understandings and theological reflection. González and Pérez summarize: "Once theology acknowledges the limits of its own contextuality, it can begin to hear what others are saying from other perspectives, and its own understanding of the gospel is thereby enriched."[*]

[*] Ibid., 30.

27. THEOLOGY AND SCIENCE

There have been many conflicts and misunderstandings through the centuries about theology and science. The term *science* describes a systematized approach to knowledge. We speak today of various kinds of sciences, such as the natural sciences and the social sciences. These embrace a number of different fields of study, from biology to psychology to sociology to zoology.

Some have looked at history and claimed that there has been "warfare" between science and theology. *A History of the Warfare of Science with Theology in Christendom* was the title of an 1896 book by Andrew Dickson White (1832–1918), president and professor of history at Cornell University, with chapter titles that included "From Creation to Evolution," "From Genesis to Geology," and "From Miracles to Medicine." White argued there was an inherent conflict between science and religion and that history showed that negative results followed when religion tried to interfere with science. Earlier, John William Draper's *History of the Conflict between Religion and Science* (1874) had also advocated this theory.

In the 1920s and '30s, the fundamentalist-modernist controversy in the United States raised issues of whether scientific theories like evolution were contrary to Christian faith. A major event was the "Monkey Trial" in Tennessee in which high school biology teacher John Scopes was put on trial for teaching evolution in the classroom.

In recent years, writers such as Richard Dawkins, Sam Harris, and Christopher Hitchens have fashioned a "new atheism" in which they have argued that religion is the cause of many of the world's problems. Some of these writers are scientists who disparage theology on the basis of their scientific viewpoints.

Other scientists and theologians have approached the relationship between theology and science differently. The following are common models:

- **Conflict**—when either discipline threatens to take over the legitimate concerns of the other. For example: John William Draper and Andrew Dickson White's conflict thesis.
- **Independence**—treating each discipline as a separate realm of enquiry. For example: Stephen Jay Gould's "Non-Overlapping Magisteria" (NOMA).
- **Dialogue**—suggesting that each field has things to say to each other about phenomena in which their interests overlap. For example, William G. Pollard's studies in *Physicist and Christian: A Dialogue between the Communities*.
- **Integration**—aiming to unify both fields into a single discourse. For example: Pierre Teilhard de Chardin's "Omega point" and Ian Barbour's sympathy toward process philosophy/process theology.[*]

Some alternative typologies are these:

- **Conflict**—the conviction that science and religion are fundamentally irreconcilable.
- **Contrast**—the claim that there can be no genuine conflict, since religion and science are each responding to radically different questions.
- **Contact**—an approach that looks for dialogue, interaction, and possible consonance between science and religion, and especially for ways in which science shapes religious and theological understanding.

[*] See "Relationship between Science and Religion," *Wikipedia*, http://en.wikipedia.org/wiki/relationship_between_religion_and_science from which this list is taken.

- **Confirmation**—a somewhat quieter but extremely important perspective that highlights the ways in which, at a very deep level, religion supports and nourishes the entire scientific enterprise.[*]

These descriptions indicate that some seek a way for theology and science to exist mutually without elements of conflict. A number of theologians hold to the "independence" or "contrast" models here to indicate that science and theology deal with two different kinds of questions. Science asks, "How?" Theology asks, "Why?" The theologian can look to science to provide descriptions of the natural world or of observable phenomena. The scientist can look to theology to describe the nature of the realities that are observed, from the point of view of understandings of God or, in the case of Christianity, the Christian theological tradition. Since theology is the study of God, God as a reality is of a completely different nature than the phenomena that are studied in science. Since the objects of study are different, each approach must use the methods that are appropriate for the type of study in which it engages. Science uses the scientific method; theology uses a theological method that accords with the God who is being studied. In the Christian tradition, this God is the God of the Hebrew and Christian Scriptures, known most fully in Jesus Christ.

Since all truth is God's truth, it is important for theology and science to recognize the nature of each approach to truth. The conflicts of the past do not need to be played out in each new generation.

[*] See John F. Haught, *Science and Religion: From Conflict to Conversation* (Mahwah, N.J.: Paulist Press, 1995), 9, following Ian G. Barbour. On one aspect of the science and religion question, see Haught, *God after Darwin: A Theology of Evolution* (Boulder, CO: Westview Press, 2000), and Haught, *Making Sense of Evolution: Darwin, God, and the Drama of Life* (Louisville, KY: Westminster John Knox Press, 2010).

VI. A BIT OF HISTORY

28. DEVELOPMENTS IN THEOLOGY: ZIGS AND ZAGS

Theology develops. All the theological knowledge we have today didn't exist ten years or ten centuries ago. As in other fields of study, the insights of earlier figures provide a basis by which later theologians develop ideas further.

So it is possible to study the history of Christian theology. Particularly on difficult and controversial issues, we see that the history of theology is not one straight or smooth line. It has traveled more in zigs and zags. It goes one way for a while and then another—and then moves out into another direction.

For example, as the church was trying to understand who Jesus Christ was, a number of theological proposals were suggested. Some theologians expressed a belief in Jesus as a divine-type being. Others said that Jesus was a real person. As they debated and the church considered a number of formulations, at points those who emphasized the divine dimensions of Jesus were predominant. Then things would shift toward formulations that emphasized Jesus' common humanity with others. Back and forth things went. Eventually, the church came to decide that both dimensions must be honored fully. So Jesus Christ is proclaimed as truly human and truly divine. This is sometimes called the christological mystery—how one person can be both divine and human at the same time. In struggling with this issue, the church went back and forth as theological statements zigged and zagged.

The "new" is not always better in theology. All theological statements must be judged in relation to many factors. But we can trace the development of Christian theology as theologians describe the realities of Christian faith with different thoughts and language. The "zigzag" path keeps us always alert for new insights while also calling us to recognize that new formulations need to be assessed in relation to what has gone before in the development of theology.

29. MAIN MOVES IN THEOLOGY (DEVELOPMENT OF DOCTRINES)

Christian doctrines develop. Doctrines are "teachings" (Lat. *doctrina*) the Christian church has embraced through the years as accurate understandings of what the Bible teaches and what the church should believe.

The doctrines are human formulations about Christian beliefs on a variety of subjects, such as the Bible, God, Jesus Christ, humanity, salvation, and sacraments. Theologians write their understandings of various doctrines. Churches that use confessions of faith or creeds rely on those documents to provide a clear statement of what they believe.

All creeds and confessions are historical documents. They are written in different times and places. They reflect many aspects of the writers, including language, culture, philosophical influences, and social location. The ways in which doctrines are articulated or written are always conditioned by these factors.

Doctrines develop over time. This development occurs as theologians write and others respond; documents are written, critiqued, and rewritten. As understandings emerge through dialogue, and even controversies, new insights are developed and incorporated into Christian understanding. This has been true throughout the history of the church, and it continues in various ways today.

Here are some of the "main moves" in the development of doctrine throughout the different periods of the church's life. Many of these developments took shape through theological controversies. In many cases, there were historical, political, or cultural factors that strongly influenced the positions being taken. The zigzag pattern that emerges as the result of controversy may lead to further controversies!

Outline of Some Main Moves in Theology

    I. The Trinity—Who is God?
        A. God is one
        B. God is three

   II. Christology—Who is Jesus Christ?
        A. Fully God
        B. Fully human

  III. Ecclesiology—What is the church?
        A. Those who lapse from the faith
        B. The church as the mystical body of Christ

  IV. Anthropology—What is humanity?
        A. The image of God
        B. Free will

   V. Soteriology—How are we saved?
        A. Different images of salvation
        B. The relation of faith and works

  VI. Authority—Where is authority?
        A. Canon, creeds, and councils
        B. Scripture and tradition

 VII. Sacraments—What are the sacraments?
        A. Definition and number of sacraments
        B. The nature of baptism
        C. The nature of the Lord's Supper

VIII. Eschatology—What is the reign of God?
        A. The millennium
        B. The nature of Christian hope[*]

---

[*] This outline basically follows the chapters in my book *Theological Turning Points: Major Issues in Christian Thought* (Atlanta: John Knox Press, 1988).

30. A ROMP THROUGH THE HISTORY OF THEOLOGY

It is useful to look at the history of theology in various periods. These are admittedly arbitrary in the ways they are designated, but they have been used for a long time. The periods provide a convenient way of looking at a slice of theological history with an eye toward seeing what main developments were occurring.

Patristic Period (c. AD 100–600)

The period of the development of the early Christian church is called the patristic period or the period of the "fathers." It was an era in which a number of important theologians were developing theological understandings to help the church find its way through vital issues (see chap. 33). Key topics include:

- **Spread of the church.** The early Christian church grew from its roots in Palestine (particularly around Jerusalem) and began to spread to neighboring areas. Early Christian missionaries preached the gospel throughout the Mediterranean world and into the imperial capital of Rome. The church in Rome took on more prominence in the early centuries, but tensions emerged with the church at Constantinople.

- **Important regions.** Several regions emerged as areas where theological discussions and debates took on special significance.

- **Alexandria.** This city in Egypt became dominant in the area of education. It had a world-famous library. It was a center of Platonism, which influenced the theology developed there. In particular, views of who Jesus Christ was (Christology) and how best to interpret Scripture (emphasis on the use of allegory) were features of the Alexandrian tradition. Its leading theologian was Origen (c. 185–254).

- **Antioch.** This city in the region of Cappadocia (modern-day Turkey) was where "the disciples were first called 'Christians'" (Acts 11:26). The church there was begun by Paul and Barnabas. Antioch became a prime center of Christian thought. Its particular approach in the early centuries affected understandings of Christology and biblical interpretation, particularly its emphasis on the natural sense of Scripture. Antioch's leading theologians were John Chrysostom (c. 347–407) and the Cappadocian Fathers: Basil of Caesarea (330–379), Gregory of Nyssa (335–395), and Gregory of Nazianzus (329–390).

- **North Africa.** The city of Carthage in western North Africa at one time vied with Rome as the preeminent city of the Mediterranean world. The leading theologian from this region was Augustine of Hippo (354–430).

- **Development of Christian doctrine.** The early Christian church spent its first several centuries trying to understand and articulate its faith in ways that were coherent and understandable. A number of church councils were held in which theological issues were debated and theological formulations put forth. Important doctrines that developed during the patristic period include the Trinity and Christology.

The patristic period is considered to have ended with the Council of Chalcedon (451) where the church formulated a detailed statement of its understanding of who Jesus Christ is.

Medieval Period (451–1500)

Historians used to speak of the years between the fall of Rome in 410 until about the year 1000 as the "Dark Ages." The term pointed to a lack of positive cultural developments, coupled with unrest and instability. But throughout those centuries, the Christian church continued, the Scriptures were copied and passed on, and faith was maintained.

The early Middle Ages were marked by the beginning of political stability and by new developments in philosophical and theological work. As the period continued, the Renaissance ("rebirth") produced a flurry of learning and developments that anticipated later directions that are still important today.

Here are three of the significant movements of the period:

- **Monasticism.** Monks who took vows and lived apart from the world in monasteries helped keep faith and learning alive during this period. In c. 540, St. Benedict (c. 480– c. 550) drew up his famous "Rule" to give structure and order to monastic life. It became the primary form for communal monastic life, and from the eighth through the twelfth centuries, Benedictine monasticism was the main expression of religious life in the West. In the eleventh through the fourteenth centuries, new monastic orders arose, following the Rule of St. Benedict. These included the Cistercian order and the Carthusian order, which featured a more reclusive approach.

- **Scholasticism.** The primary approach for learning developed in medieval university settings. It featured philosophical methods and the use of reason and logic to provide rational justification for philosophical and theological positions, which were presented systematically in a logical fashion. The goal was to achieve a thorough and comprehensive picture of theology. Leading figures were Thomas

Aquinas (1225–1274), Duns Scotus (c. 1265–1308), and William of Ockham (c. 1288–c. 1348).

- **Humanism.** The scholars in this movement sought to study classical languages and sources to recover the wisdom of the early period in order to gain eloquence in spoken and written communication. The motto of the humanists was *Ad fontes*, or "back to the sources." Humanism was a cultural and educational movement interested in how to express and present ideas. There were many humanists who applied their perspectives to Christianity. They sought to recover the wisdom of early Christian traditions and to read ancient texts with concern for their linguistic, historical, and cultural contexts. Leading figures of humanism included Marsilio Ficino (1433–1499), Rudolph Agricola (1443–1485), Giovanni Pico della Mirandola (1463–1494), Desiderius Erasmus (c. 1466–1536), as well as the Christian theologians Huldrych Zwingli (1484–1531) and John Calvin (1509–1564).

The Middle Ages also included a key event in Christian history. In 1054 the church in the West split from the church in the East. The theological reason for the split was over an understanding of the "procession" of the Holy Spirit. In the Trinity, does the Holy Spirit "proceed" from the Father and the Son (Western view) or only from the Father (Eastern view)? While this seems like a squabble over words, the issue does have some important theological implications. The Latin term *filioque* means "and the Son." Since the ninth century, Western Christians had typically altered the Nicene Creed with this Latin phrase to say that the Holy Spirit proceeded "from the Father and from the Son." This became known as the "double procession." Eastern Christians rejected this theological understanding, however.

The ecclesiastical reason for the split related to the growth of the papacy and the power of the pope in the Western churches. Eastern churches looked to the patriarch of Constantinople as the leader of the church.

Eastern churches are often called "Byzantine" churches, after the Greek city of Byzantium, which the Emperor Constantine chose as his capital (330) and which was later renamed "Constantinople." These churches became known as "Eastern Orthodox."

The East-West split is the biggest divide among Christians. While dialogues and conversations have occurred through the years, the churches in these two main branches of Christianity have not reunited.

Reformation and Post-Reformation Periods (1500–1700)

The Protestant Reformation changed the religious landscape of Europe and unleashed repercussions that continue to this day. The word "Protestant" comes from the Latin *protestare*, which means "to witness." Protestants sought to witness to their Christian faith. Protestant reformers who set out to initiate reform of the Roman Catholic Church found that their own theological ideas were adopted by followers far beyond their own local areas. The religious and theological revolution of the sixteenth century and its aftermath significantly shaped institutions and church traditions with which we are familiar today.

Three main "streams" flowed from the Protestant Reformation in the sixteenth century:

- **Lutheran.** The Protestant Reformation began when Martin Luther, an Augustinian monk, produced his Ninety-five Theses, a list of statements that expressed his concerns about the teachings and practices of the Roman Catholic Church. Luther sought church reform from within, but the pope excommunicated him. Through Luther's many writings, however, his ideas spread, and large numbers of people began to follow his approach to Christianity. The churches established after Luther's death are called "Lutheran," and the theological tradition that emerged is called "Lutheranism."

- **Reformed.** Two Swiss theologians initiated an alternative vision to Luther's, while also critiquing the Roman Catholic Church. Huldrych Zwingli in Zurich sought theological and liturgical reform. John Calvin in Geneva wrote extensive biblical commentaries, sermons, theological treatises, and letters. These and his main theological work, *Institutes of the Christian Religion*, were tremendously important to those who followed this path. "Reformed" Christians sought to reform the church in accordance with the word of God in Scripture even more thoroughly than the Lutherans.

- **Anabaptist.** A third stream of the Protestant Reformation also rejected Roman Catholicism but could not follow either Lutheranism or the Reformed. "Anabaptists" got their name from their rejection of infant baptism, a practice sanctioned by the other two Protestant streams (as well as the Roman Catholic Church). Anabaptists believed only adult or "believer's baptism" was valid. They also rejected the use of oaths and participating in civil government. Leading figures were Thomas Müntzer (1488–1525), Melchior Hoffman (1495–1543), and Menno Simons (1496–1561).

Protestantism spread throughout Europe, into the British Isles and to the New World. The formation of many denominations was the result. Church bodies often split over a variety of issues, usually theological in nature. From the outside, many of these issues seem small and essentially unimportant.

To those involved in the controversies, the issues took on great importance. They were so important that the body of Christ, the church, was split. In contemporary times, while church splits continue to occur, many Christians wish that a number of historic breaks in the body of Christ could be healed and overcome (see chap. 16).

Modern Period (1700–Present)

Since the Reformation, the history of the church has been marked by the spread of Christianity throughout the world and the recognition of the global nature of Christianity. Main movements include the following:

- **Enlightenment.** Intellectuals in eighteenth-century Europe were convinced that truth could be obtained only by the powers of reason, observation, and experiment. This perspective challenged Christianity as various thinkers sought to find intellectual roots for religion or to jettison religion altogether as mere superstition or as the projection of human needs and desires. Leading figures included Baruch Spinoza (1632–1677), John Locke (1632–1704), David Hume (1711–1776), and Immanuel Kant (1724–1804).

- **Liberal Protestantism.** Intellectual attacks on religion in eighteenth- and nineteenth-century Europe, along with the findings of the natural sciences, such as the Darwinian theory of evolution, opened a wide gap between many people and the Christian faith. Liberal Protestantism arose in response to this chasm. Friedrich Schleiermacher and Albrecht Ritschl provided theological systems that sought to locate the essence of religious faith within human experience and to jettison or reinterpret Christian teachings to align them with what was known of the contemporary world at that time. Main emphases in liberal theology were optimism about the human ability to progress and prosper, along with a focus on ethics as values that would move society along toward the kingdom of God. Leading figures were Schleiermacher (1768–1834), William Ellery Channing (1780–1842), Ritschl (1822–1889), Adolf von Harnack (1851–1930), and Harry Emerson Fosdick (1878–1969).

- **Neo-orthodoxy.** Karl Barth was a Swiss theologian who reacted against the liberal theology of his teachers by "rediscovering" the biblical and Reformation insight that theology is centered in God, not humanity. The aftermath of World War I brought disillusionment with liberal theology's optimism, and Barth proclaimed the "Godness of God," who stands separated as the "wholly Other" from humans, because of human sin. Barth's theology centered in Jesus Christ as the "elect" one in whom God has reached out to save the world and to establish reconciliation and faith. Barth's views were influential in America from the 1940s through the 1960s and are of continuing interest today. In addition to Barth (1886–1968), leading figures in neo-orthodoxy include H. Emil Brunner (1889–1966) and Reinhold Niebuhr (1892–1971).

- **Fundamentalism.** In the United States, one response to liberal theology and emerging secular culture was a reassertion of Protestant doctrines and values. This led to the fundamentalist/modernist controversy during the 1920s in which Darwinism became a central issue and the Scopes "monkey trial" over evolution became a symbol of the clash of these two differing worldviews and theological perspectives. The literal inerrancy of Scripture, the blood atonement of Jesus Christ, and the premillennial return of Christ were some of the central theological "fundamentals." Leading figures were William Bell Riley (1861–1947), Bob Jones

(1883–1968), John R. Rice (1895–1980), and Jerry L. Falwell (1933–2007).

- **Evangelicalism.** A reaction to the strong positions of fundamentalism set in during the early 1950s when some conservative Protestants continued to maintain central tenets of the Christian faith but in a wider, more irenic sense than that of contemporary fundamentalists. Emphasis was placed on the death of Christ, conversion as being "born again" and a badge of Christian identity, Scripture as authoritative, and spreading the gospel through evangelism. Evangelicals also broke with fundamentalists in that they sought a more socially engaged rather than anticultural stance. Leading figures were Carl F. H. Henry (1913–2003), Billy Graham (1919–), Edward J. Carnell (1919–1967), and Donald G. Bloesch (1928–2010).

- **Roman Catholicism—Vatican II.** Growing secularism in Western cultures led Pope John XXIII (1958–1963) to convene the Second Vatican Council (1962–1965) to consider updating the church's agenda. A wide range of topics was addressed, and wide-ranging changes in the church were instituted. Emphasis on the church as a believing community instead of primarily a hierarchy, a stronger role for laity, and emphasis on the social dimensions of Christian faith and on ecumenism were some of the important outcomes of the council.

- **Process theology.** In this theological movement emerging from the works of Alfred North Whitehead and Charles Hartshorne, reality is perceived to be in a constant emergent "becoming," rather than in a static situation of "being." The divine (God) participates in the emerging world and works cooperatively with persons who act freely and creatively. God is a God of relational power and not absolute control. Jesus responded fully to the call of God and in every minute identified with God. Leading figures include Alfred North Whitehead (1861–1947), Charles Hartshorne (1897–2000), John B. Cobb Jr. (1925–), David Ray Griffin (1939–), and Marjorie Hewitt Suchocki (1943–).

- **Liberation theologies.** A number of twentieth-century theological movements presented the Christian gospel as "liberation," and many of them continue on the contemporary scene (see chap. 36). The gospel liberates from all forms of societal and cultural oppression—economic, spiritual, political, and social. Emphasis is on "praxis" (the putting into practice of a theory or belief) or the concrete ways in which liberation of the oppressed, especially the poor, is carried out. Leading figures are José Miguez Bonino (1924–), Gustavo Gutiérrez (1928–), Hugo Assmann (1933–2008), and Leonardo Boff (1938–).

- **Postmodernism.** The belief that Western cultures have moved beyond Enlightenment modernism and toward a rejection of seeking "objective truth" describes postmodernism. Claims for universality, trust in the powers of reason to provide a foundation for all people to build on, and rejection of the possibility of finding the intentions of an author of a text are also characteristics of postmodernism. Some believe no meaning at all can be found in texts, since to assert a meaning is also to assert an "authority" over others that stifles their creativity and their right freely to interpret for themselves. Leading figures include Jean Baudrillard (1929–2007), Jacques Derrida (1930–2004), Michel Foucault (1926–1984), and Richard Rorty (1931–2007).

The spread of Christianity throughout the globe has meant that people outside the traditional "centers" of Christian theology—Europe and North America—now do theology in their own contexts.

In the last hundred years, Christianity has grown in some places on the earth and retracted in others. This has been called a "macroreformation." There has been a large demographic shift on a global level. As one scholar put it, speaking of the relation of the first half of the twentieth century to the second half, "The typical late twentieth-century Christian was no longer a European man, but a Latin American or African woman."* Another was even more direct: "The centers of the church's universality [are] no longer in Geneva, Rome, Athens, Paris, London, New York, but Kinshasa, Buenos Aires, Addis Ababa and Manila."† Where the church is, theological reflection is found. New and different theological voices are being heard today, sums up Justo L. González, "from quarters that have not been the traditional centers of theological inquiry, and from people who have not been among the traditional theological leaders."‡

In the broad sense, "global theology" does not mean establishing one "universal theology" that will speak equally well to all persons in all places at all times. That is impossible! Rather, "global theology" points to theologies arising from various local contexts as they are in dialogue with each other. Theological traditions and the church's theological heritage continue to have their place and play their roles. The insights of major theologians from the past still have power to speak today. But now, write William A. Dyrness and Veli-Matti Kärk-käinen, "newer voices are adding their accents to the Christian conversation."§ This makes global theology exciting!

* Dana L. Robert, "Shifting Southward: Global Christianity since 1945," cited in the introduction to *Global Dictionary of Theology*, ed. William A. Dyrness and Veli-Matti Kärkkäinen (Downers Grove, IL: InterVarsity Press, 2008), ix.

† John Mbiti, cited in Dyrness and Kärkkäinen, *Global Dictionary of Theology*, ix.

‡ Justo L. González, *Mañana: Christian Theology from a Hispanic Perspective* (Nashville: Abingdon Press, 1990), 49.

§ Dyrness and Kärkkäinen, *Global Dictionary of Theology*, xii.

VII. DOING THEOLOGY

31. WHAT IS THEOLOGICAL METHOD?

The word "method" comes from the Greek word *methodos*, which means "a way through." It is the process or procedure by which something is done. A surgical method is a way in which surgery is done. Theological method is a plan or set of principles by which the practice of theology is carried out.

To decide on a theological method means making a lot of decisions. Our decision about how to approach or tackle a theological issue or the study of theology itself rests on a number of questions. Here are a few:

- What is our view of revelation? Do we believe God can be known? Has God been revealed? If so, where and how?

- How do we know? In what ways can we know theological truth? Is it through revelation (in nature or Scripture), through reason (our abilities to think), or through experience (in a relationship with a divine person)?

- What is our view of language? Do we believe human language is an adequate and appropriate means by which the deep realities of theology can be expressed or conveyed?

- What is our view of God? Who is this God? What is God's nature? Is there a God to study?

- What is our view of humanity? What abilities do humans have that enable them to do theology or to come to decisions about what is true?

32. THREE MAJOR THEOLOGICAL METHODS

Theologians have used a number of theological methods throughout history. Three of the most important are these:

- **I believe in order to understand.** This approach to theology is associated with the great early church theologian Augustine (354–430). Augustine said, "In matters of great importance, pertaining to divinity, we must first believe before we seek to know. Otherwise the words of the prophet would be vain, where he says: 'Except ye believe ye shall not understand.'"*

  What it means: Augustine meant that we know God through faith as God is revealed to us. Faith is a gift from God. Once we believe in God, our faith will impel us to desire further understanding or knowledge of God. Our knowledge enables our faith to grow, and our faith leads us to seek further knowledge.

- **Reason leads to faith.** This approach to theology is associated with the great medieval theologian Thomas Aquinas (1225–1274) and his followers. Aquinas wrote, "Sensible things, from which the human reason takes the origin of its knowledge, retain within themselves some sort of trace of a likeness to God."†

---

* Cited in Jack B. Rogers and Donald K. McKim, *The Authority and Interpretation of the Bible: An Historical Approach*, expanded ed. (Eugene, OR: Wipf & Stock, 1999), 23. This book shows the importance of the theological methods in relation to the doctrine of Scripture.

† Cited in ibid., 46.

What it means: Aquinas believed that through human reason and various rational arguments, one can conclude that God exists. One can begin with human thought, establish that there is a God, and from there believe certain things about God. Aquinas knew that reason could not say all there is to say about God. For that we need revelation. But his method means that Christian faith is a two-step process: First, one uses reason to prove that God exists, then one goes on to faith, which for Aquinas meant to believe what the church teaches about God.

- **I believe in order to experience.** This approach to theology is associated with the great mystical theologian Bernard of Clairvaux (1090–1153). Bernard wrote, "Let us model ourselves on Scripture which expresses the wisdom hidden in mystery in our own words: when Scripture portrays God for us it suggests Him in terms of our own feelings."*

  What it means: Bernard and others emphasized that the goal of theology was to bring us into a "mystical" experience. This is a direct awareness of God that does not come through reason or faith but is the direct work of the Holy Spirit as a person contemplates God.

* Cited in ibid., 51.

33. BIG-TIME THEOLOGIANS DOING THEOLOGY

There have been a number of theological giants through the centuries. Not all their ideas have always been accepted by their peers—or by the Christian church—as being "correct." But these persons have contributed to the ongoing story of Christian theology, and their ideas continue to be important today.

Early Church Period

- **Justin Martyr (c. 100–165).** The first apologist for Christianity, Justin wrote to defend the Christian faith against non-Christians, especially philosophers. He believed philosophy was just a shadow of the truth that Christianity, as the true wisdom, provides. His idea of *logos spermatikos* ("seed-bearing word") was that God prepared the way for Jesus Christ through hints of truth that emerged in classical philosophy.

- **Irenaeus of Lyon (c. 130–c. 200).** A strong defender of Christianity against Gnosticism, which taught that a "secret knowledge" was needed for salvation, Irenaeus believed that Jesus Christ was the "second Adam" who reversed the curse of the "first Adam" by bringing redemption from sin. This idea is called recapitulation. It means that Jesus Christ recapitulates in his life and death all the things that Adam lost with his fall into sin.

- **Tertullian (c. 160–c. 225).** This North African theologian defended the unity of the Old and New Testaments against Marcion, who denied the Old Testament should be used by Christians. Tertullian rejected the value of philosophy and denied the place of wisdom outside the church. He was the first theologian to write in Latin. Tertullian developed the use of the term "person" to describe the members of the Trinity.

- **Origen (c. 185–c. 254).** A major theologian from Alexandria, Origen used allegory to interpret many biblical passages. He believed that God will restore the whole of creation to its original spiritual state. He also argued for universalism, the view that all humanity (including Satan) will be saved. His *On First Principles* was the first systematic theology. A number of his ideas were condemned by later church councils.

- **Arius (c. 270–336).** A pastor and theologian from Alexandria, Arius held views that led to debates over the Trinity. These views were condemned by the Councils of Nicaea (325) and Constantinople (381). Arius believed that only God the Father is eternal and that the Son is a creature, the product of the Father's will. Arianism continued to be expressed in various forms to the end of the sixth century.

- **Athanasius (c. 296–c. 373).** This tireless defender of the view that God became a person in Jesus Christ rejected the view of Arius that the Son was a creature of the Father, making him not fully God. If so, then the incarnation was of little importance and salvation could not be accomplished. Athanasius stressed Jesus Christ as truly God and truly human. Salvation is possible because of Jesus' complete identification with humans in his humanity, and Jesus has the power to save sinful humans because he is truly God.

- **Cappadocian Fathers (Gregory of Nazianzus [329–390], Basil of Caesarea [330–379], Gregory of Nyssa [335–395]).** These three important theologians from Cappadocia in

Asia Minor helped in the development of orthodox views of the Trinity in the Eastern church. Their writings emphasized that the three members of the Trinity were distinct from each other. This contrasted with the views of other theologians, especially Augustine, who emphasized their unity in the Godhead.

- **Augustine (354–430).** A major theologian of the Western church, Augustine's ideas were highly influential for centuries. He contributed to the doctrines of the Trinity, sin and grace, and the church and sacraments. He also provided a panoramic view of God's work in the world in his great book *The City of God*.

Medieval Theologians

- **Boethius (c. 480–525).** This important philosopher and scholar famously defined a person as "the individual substance of a rational nature," which was important in definitions of the Trinity. His work *The Consolation of Philosophy* indicated the importance of philosophy to help the soul come to a vision of God.

- **Anselm (1033–1109).** This Archbishop of Canterbury saw faith as the precondition for using reason rightly and cast many of his theological works in the form of prayers. His argument for the existence of God defines God as "something than which nothing greater can be thought" (*Proslogion*), and his *Cur Deus Homo* (*Why God Become a Human*) was the first systematic treatment of the atonement, interpreting the death of Christ in terms of "satisfaction."

- **Peter Abelard (1079–1142/3).** A versatile theologian, Abelard questioned the content of Christian faith to understand it more fully. He rejected Anselm's satisfaction view of the atonement and stressed Christ's suffering and death as the great example of God's love for humanity, which should then evoke responses of gratitude and love in believers.

- **Thomas Aquinas (1225–1274).** The greatest medieval theologian, Aquinas developed the famous "five ways" for establishing the existence of God, based on reason. There is an "analogy of being" between God and the world, a continuity that exists because God's being is in the world. Thus, humans can use reason to establish God's existence. But God's revelation is necessary to go beyond what reason can know. Thomas wrote "895 lectures on Aristotle, 803 on the Scriptures, 850 chapters on the Gospels, and 2,652 'articles,'" or discussions of specific questions, in the *Summa Theologiae*, his classic work.[*]

- **Duns Scotus (c. 1265–1308).** This sharp-minded theologian said that God's "will" took precedence over God's "intellect" (against Aquinas), a view known as voluntarism. Less emphasis is thus placed on human reason, and more on obeying God's will.

- **William of Ockham (c. 1285–1347).** William also stressed the priority of God's will over God's intellect. His "Ockham's razor" was a principle that said all hypotheses that are not necessary can be eliminated. He eliminated the notion of universals, or general concepts, arguing that only individual things exist and are directly known by the mind. This view is called nominalism.

Reformation Era (Sixteenth Century)

- **Teresa of Ávila (1515–1582).** A Spanish Carmelite nun and reformer who was the first woman declared a Doctor of the Church (by Pope Paul VI in 1970), Teresa is known for her

[*] Justo L. González, ed., *The Westminster Dictionary of Theologians* (Louisville, KY: Westminster John Knox Press, 2006), 332.

teachings about the ascent of the soul to God in four stages. Her writings on mental prayer are significant. She also emphasized love for others and the unity of body and soul. She believed heaven would consist of the enjoyment of God and continuing relations with friends.

- **Martin Luther (1483–1546).** This Augustinian monk began the Protestant Reformation with his Ninety-five Theses, which sought reform of the Roman Catholic Church. Luther translated the Bible into German and wrote many theological books and biblical commentaries. His key insight was that salvation is a gift of God, received by faith. This doctrine of salvation by grace through faith spurred his followers (Lutherans) to spread his work throughout Europe.

- **Huldrych Zwingli (1484–1531).** This Swiss reformer began church reform in Zurich. His insights, along with those of John Calvin, helped initiate what became the Reformed branch of the Protestant Reformation. Zwingli stressed election and predestination and also had a distinctive view of the Lord's Supper. He argued there was no "real presence" of Christ in the Supper and that "This is my body" (1 Cor. 11:24) should be interpreted as "This *means*, or this *represents*, my body," a view sometimes called "memorialism."

- **Menno Simons (1496–1561).** A leading figure in the Anabaptist branch of the Protestant Reformation, Simons rejected infant baptism in favor of adult or "believer's" baptism along with the independence of each local church congregation and the rejection of Christian participation in government. Simons escaped martyrdom, the fate of many Anabaptist leaders. Thus, he was able to be influential among Anabaptist groups in northern Europe. His influence was especially strong toward their adopting pacifist views.

- **Philipp Melanchthon (1497–1560).** This German humanist scholar and reformer, known as the "Teacher of

Germany," was a close collaborator of Luther's and was his theological successor. Melanchthon's *Loci communes* (1521) was an important work for the spread of Reformation ideas. Melanchthon wrote the Augsburg Confession (1530), which became an important document in the Lutheran theological tradition. Melanchthon was involved in numerous disputes but sought ecumenical agreement where possible.

- **John Calvin (1509–1564).** A French humanist who became committed to the reform of the Roman Catholic Church, Calvin worked as a pastor and teacher in Geneva, where he was intimately involved in the city. He became an internationally known theologian and leader, writing many biblical commentaries and theological works, the most notable being his *Institutes of the Christian Religion* (1536–1560). He stressed God's initiative in all things, including salvation. This is expressed in the doctrine of election or predestination, which emphasizes God's free decision in granting salvation to individuals through the gift of faith in Jesus Christ.

- **Theodore Beza (1519–1605).** The successor to John Calvin and the first headmaster of the Academy of Geneva (and predecessor of the University of Geneva), Beza was a humanist and poet and practiced law before becoming a Protestant. As a pastor in Geneva and the city's most prominent leader, Beza played a major role after Calvin's death. His theological writings included works on predestination, and he became an important figure in the movement toward Reformed scholasticism in the seventeenth century.

- **Francis Turretin (1623–1687).** A Reformed scholastic theologian, Turretin's three-volume theology *Institutio theologiae elenticae* (1679–1685) was of long-lasting importance in the Reformed tradition. Turretin maintained the Calvinism expressed at the Synod of Dort and held to the verbal inspiration of Scripture and the Bible's complete accuracy in all things. Turretin's *Institutio* was used as the theology textbook at Princeton Theological Seminary until the publication of Charles Hodge's *Systematic Theology* (1871–1873).

Modern Theologians

- **Jonathan Edwards (1703–1758).** Edwards is sometimes called "America's Theologian" due to his brilliance and wide-ranging importance. Though most remembered for his sermon "Sinners in the Hands of an Angry God," Edwards wrote important theological works, probing the nature of the human will, religious affections, and salvation. He also emphasized the need for visible expressions of vital Christian faith.

- **John Wesley (1703–1791).** The "Father of Methodism," Wesley was ordained in the Church of England, but after a religious conversion in which his heart was "strangely warmed," he began a long life of preaching and writing in which he traveled some 250,000 miles and preached at least forty thousand sermons. A holder of Arminian views, Wesley emphasized the need for human response to the gospel.

- **Friedrich Schleiermacher (1768–1834).** The "Father of Modern Theology" was a preacher in the Evangelical Church of the Prussian Union and a professor of theology at the University of Berlin. His work *The Christian Faith* (1821–1822) conveyed his views. Schleiermacher stressed religious experience as a sense of absolute dependence on the divine as the basis for Christian faith. For Schleiermacher, Christ lived this consciousness fully and spread it to others, becoming the Savior. Doctrines are historical products to be revised and continually reformulated.

- **Søren Kierkegaard (1813–1855).** This Danish theologian was an important thinker whose influence emerged later in the work of scholars such as Rudolf Bultmann and Karl Barth and the so-called existentialist theologians. Kierkegaard saw Christian faith as antithetical to human reason, stressing the "infinite qualitative difference" between God and humanity, and the paradox of God and humanity being united in the person of Jesus Christ. Truth must be acted upon, not just intellectually believed. He emphasized the "leap of faith."

- **Albrecht Ritschl (1822–1889).** Ritschl was an important architect of German liberal theology. In *Justification and Reconciliation* (1870–1874), he focused on Jesus, whose life and message attempted to establish the kingdom of God. The kingdom comes in Jesus (justification) and can be appropriated by his disciples through lives of moral action lived in love. This ethical life in society is to give expression to the kingdom in society and its institutions (sanctification). Ritschl stressed practical Christianity and lives of action.

- **P. T. Forsyth (1848–1921).** This British pastor and theologian criticized the dominant liberal theology of his day and wrote to establish Christ and the cross as the core realities of Christian faith. Forsyth's theology also emphasized ministry and sacraments as key elements for the church. He embraced the critical study of the Bible but rejected optimistic liberal views of the nature of humanity, stressing the need for God's grace in the gospel of Christ and the victory of God's love in Christ, expressed in the cross.

- **Adolf von Harnack (1851–1930).** This German theologian and church historian wrote more than 1,600 books and articles. His multivolume history of dogma displayed his wide learning. His lectures in 1899–1900 at the University of Berlin, where he taught, drew large crowds and were published in English as *What Is Christianity?* Harnack sought the original message of Jesus as the essence of Christianity, rejecting the layers of "Hellenist spirit" that led to later doctrines that hide the basic simplicity of Jesus' message of the coming kingdom of God, the fatherhood of God, the value of the human soul, and the commandment of love.

- **Paul Tillich (1886–1965).** Tillich, a German theologian who moved to the United States in 1933, became one of the most influential Protestant theologians of the twentieth century. He argued that theology should seek a "correlation" between Christian faith and contemporary culture. In Tillich's theology, God is the "ground of being" who is found through ultimate questions. God is "being itself" and not "a being." God is revealed in Jesus the Christ who is the "new being" and in whom the estrangement and disruption of human life—that is, sin—can be overcome. The Christ offers reconciliation, creativity, and the transformation of existence in the new age of the kingdom of God.

- **Karl Barth (1886–1968).** The major Protestant theologian of the twentieth century, Barth rejected the liberal theology of his teachers and, because of his Scripture studies, emphasized the "wholly otherness of God" (Kierkegaard). Humans are sinful, yet God has loved the world in Jesus Christ, who is the "elect God and elect man." Through Christ the world has been reconciled to God, solely by God's grace. Barth reoriented the doctrine of election in this affirmation, in which God provides for the world's salvation in Christ, a reality that is recognized by the work of the Holy Spirit to bring faith to undeserving sinners.

- **Emil Brunner (1889–1966).** Brunner was a Swiss theologian who, with Karl Barth, is associated with neo-orthodoxy and the twentieth-century rejection of liberal theology. Brunner broke with Barth in a famous dispute on "natural theology" and whether there is a revelation of God outside Jesus Christ. Brunner maintained that the will of God can be known through the church, in history, and in the image of God. The Bible is the source of revelation but is an indirect witness to God's Word in Jesus Christ and is not infallible or inerrant itself.

- **Reinhold Niebuhr (1892–1971).** Niebuhr was an important American theologian and ethicist whose influence continues today in a variety of places. He taught at Union Theological Seminary in New York for many years. He is associated with "political realism" and theologically took an Augustinian view of human nature—that humans are sinful and cannot ourselves alter our attitudes of pride and idolatry. The love of God known in Jesus Christ liberates us from sin to live in the approximation of the love we know and as an impetus to improve human life and social conditions. All human institutions will be sin-affected, but in freedom we can pursue social good, placing ultimate confidence in the kingdom of God.

- **Karl Rahner (1904–1984).** Perhaps the most significant Roman Catholic theologian of the twentieth century, Rahner was a German Jesuit whose wide-ranging writings portrayed God as "mystery" and humans as radically free to shape and transform the natural and social world. The goal of human beings is to turn to God so that our human nature corresponds to God's nature and the realization of human nature as being truly free. Theology helps humans understand their transcendental orientation toward the mystery of God.

- **Dietrich Bonhoeffer (1906–1945).** This German Protestant theologian was executed for his participation in a plot to assassinate Adolf Hitler. His provocative writings include *The Cost of Discipleship*, where he contrasts "cheap grace" and "costly grace," the latter being the mark of genuine discipleship to Christ, since it can cost us our lives. Bonhoeffer anticipated a "world come of age" in which humans live "as though God were not there," necessitating an interpretation of Christian theology that can be compelling to people living in a secular world.

- **Edward Schillebeeckx (1914–2009).** This Roman Catholic theologian of the Dominican order was a theological expert at the Second Vatican Council, but his writings have been twice investigated by the church. He wrote many books, including *Jesus* (English trans. 1979), *Christ* (1981), and *Church* (1990), that display his desire to dialogue with biblical studies and with non-Christian religions.

- **Jürgen Moltmann (1926–).** This major German Protestant theologian came to the study of theology after over three years as a prisoner of war in Scotland, Belgium, and England. His *Theology of Hope* (1964) reoriented theology by beginning it with eschatology—and the Christian belief in the ultimate hope and transformation of the world in Jesus Christ. *The Crucified God* (1972) showed the importance of the theology of the cross in which God is revealed in Christ. Other works creatively interpret Christian doctrines, always recognizing Jesus Christ as the guide for humanity's living on the way to the promised future that God in Christ has secured.

- **Gustavo Gutiérrez (1928–).** Gutiérrez, a Peruvian Roman Catholic theologian, is one of the leaders of Latin American liberation theology. In *A Theology of Liberation* (1971), he described the God revealed in Israel and in Jesus Christ as the God who has a preferential option for the poor and who works for their liberation in human history. Liberation includes liberation from economic exploitation, political oppression, and cultural liberation. Theology reflects on "praxis" and on the actions of the church for liberation of the poor in light of God's Word. The goal is the transformation of the world and a new society.

- **Hans Küng (1928–).** This controversial Swiss theologian lost his official designation as a Roman Catholic theologian in 1979. Küng's doctoral dissertation argued that Karl Barth's view of justification and the Roman Catholic doctrine formulated at the Council of Trent were in basic agreement. Other works, such as *The Church* (1967) and *Infallible?* (1970), questioned traditional Roman views and sought reform. Other key works are *On Being a Christian* (1977), *Does God Exist?* (1980), and *Theology for the Third Millennium* (1991). Later works emphasize Christian theology as ecumenical and in dialogue with world religions.

- **Wolfhart Pannenberg (1928–).** A German Lutheran theologian who taught in Munich, Pannenberg has emphasized the interpretation of history from its end or goal, on a universal plane. History's end is found in the life, death, and resurrection of Jesus Christ, so God's revelation is found in events of history interpreted as God's actions. The resurrection is a historical event for Pannenberg that shows the "end" of history has arrived, even as historical events continue. *Jesus—God and Man* (1968) is Pannenberg's Christology and his argument for the historicity of the resurrection. He also has written a three-volume systematic theology (English trans. 1991–1998).

- **Letty Russell (1929–2007).** A Presbyterian feminist theologian, Russell taught at Yale Divinity School from 1974 until 2001. She contended the gospel of Christ was transformative and that the Bible was a book of radical freedom. In *Church in the Round: Feminist Interpretation of the Church* (1993), she proposed "leadership in the round" as an image to give laypersons greater authority in the church. Russell emphasized hospitality and partnership as important

Christian practices. Her liberationist critique of the church was rooted in historic traditions.

- **Sallie McFague (1933–).** A feminist theologian who taught at Vanderbilt University for many years, McFague initially produced works on the parables (*Speaking in Parables*, 1975) and theological language (*Metaphorical Theology*, 1982). Then followed *Models for God* (1987) and *The Body of God: An Ecological Theology* (1993). McFague's theology emphasizes liberation and resistance to the oppressions of gender, race, and class. Her emphases are on organic and social models to describe the nature of God's relationship to the world.

- **Rosemary Radford Ruether (1936–).** This important feminist theologian has written a number of books, including *Sexism and God-Talk: Toward a Feminist Theology* (1983). Here theology begins with the experience of women as the starting point for reinterpreting the Judeo-Christian tradition. The emphasis is on finding elements of liberation and prophetic insight from sacred texts. These are important in light of traditional patriarchal interpretations that reinforce domination by hierarchical powers in church and society. Dominating patriarchal systems, addressed in other writings, include environmental exploitation, colonialism, economic oppression, heterosexism, and racism.

- **Elisabeth Schüssler Fiorenza (1938–).** In her book *In Memory of Her: A Feminist Theological Reconstruction of Christian Origins* (1983), feminist theologian and biblical scholar Schüssler Fiorenza emphasizes the importance of historical contexts for biblical interpretation. She has argued that the basic insight of all liberation theologies (including feminist theologies) is that all theology is engaged either for or against the oppressed, so it is not possible to be neutral, since the world is exploitative and oppressive. Schüssler Fiorenza has taught at Harvard Divinity School.

- **David Tracy (1939–).** A Roman Catholic theologian who has taught at the University of Chicago, Tracy focuses on the ways texts, human experience, and language relate to each other in the modern and postmodern world. His important books include *Blessed Rage for Order* (1975), *The Analogical Imagination* (1981), and *Plurality and Ambiguity: Hermeneutics, Religion, Hope* (1987). Tracy has emphasized a public theology, exploring the relationships among theology, society, and politics.

VIII. THEOLOGY TODAY

34. THEOLOGY TODAY

Theology today is marked by attention both to historic traditions and to contemporary questions and issues.

The traditional elements of Christian doctrine continue to be important, both intellectually and spiritually. The ways in which the "dry bones" of older themes can be brought to life in new ways for new understandings and impact on lives continue to produce ongoing efforts by theologians. Dietrich Bonhoeffer said that the real question for theologians is not so much "Who is Jesus Christ?" but rather "Who is Jesus Christ today?" Part of the ongoing work of theology is to focus on ways in which what the church has believed and what theologians have said in the past can find new expressions in contemporary contexts.

Another dimension of theology today is dealing with the kinds of issues and questions that are posed by contemporary cultures. Theologians who focus on these tasks seek specific responses that are contextually based. The goal, as T. D. Gener explains, is to "address particular issues, questions and concerns of a particular public . . . where God's story of the world meets our big and little stories at a particular time and place." In this respect, a contextual theology "calls for a genuine give-and-take with one's culture to discern what form of the Word is appropriate for a particular time and place."*

An important part of theology seen in this light is dialogue. This is true in both local contexts and in larger theological dialogues between majority world theologians and those in Asia, Africa, or Latin America. This approach also faces the need for interpreting both the Bible and local

* T. D. Gener, "Systematic Theology Contextually Considered," in the entry on "Systematic Theology," in *Global Dictionary of Theology: A Resource for the Worldwide Church*, ed. William A. Dyrness and Veli-Matti Kärkkäinen (Downers Grove, IL: InterVarsity Press, 2008), 866.

cultures. This in turn can lead to the development of new theological "languages" and ways of expression to convey Christian truth.

So theology today faces many challenges. Theologians in the present draw on the past and move on to the future. Through it all, they do the work of theology, which is ever old and ever new.

35. BIG QUESTIONS IN THEOLOGY

Theologians have tackled big questions in theology through the centuries. They have proposed answers to the greatest issues that humans can face and contemplate.

Theological controversies have emerged when these answers have varied and when the differences in opinion were considered significant enough to warrant sharp replies or, sometimes, actions by the church. Other theological questions continue to elicit responses and a variety of opinions.

Among the big questions in theology are these:

- **What is God like?** The nature of God and the ways God works are central issues to various theological understandings—and always will be.

- **Where does evil come from?** Christian theologians have always said that God is not the author of evil. What is the origin of that which opposes God in the universe?

- **Who is Jesus Christ?** Christian theologians have adopted theological language to describe who Jesus Christ is. What are appropriate contemporary expressions of the person of Jesus Christ?

- **What is salvation?** This key theological issue has received various answers in the history of Christian theology. What does salvation look like in our contemporary world?

- **Is the church necessary?** The church emerged as the place where believers in Jesus Christ gathered in fellowship. Are today's church institutions still necessary for persons to be Christians?

- **Will all persons be saved?** Most Christian theologians and official church teachings reject the view that all persons will be saved. Is their view still seen as consistent with the Scriptures?

36. CONTEMPORARY CURRENTS IN THEOLOGY

A number of approaches to theology have developed since the 1960s. Some of them have been reactions against older, traditional theological approaches. In other instances they have emerged out of the experience of particular groups of people who have articulated theological methods and approaches that reflect the realities of their lives.

Black Theology

In the United States, black theology arose in the late 1960s and stressed the theme of liberation. Different emphases developed among black theologians, and liberation took on multiple meanings. For some, liberation is defined in relation to biblical assertions of God's liberation to the oppressed and the stories of freedom these engender. For some, liberation is a part of broader empowerment for black people. For others, liberation relates primarily to social and political philosophy and the potential for human life. Black theology has both an academic component in relation to professional theologians as well as a strong context and following in black churches. Leading figures are James H. Cone, J. Deotis Roberts, Gayraud Wilmore, Dwight Hopkins, Anthony Pinn, and James Evans.

Feminist Theology

Theological perspectives that focus on the experiences, needs, and concerns of women have developed into feminist theologies. There is a common recognition of the oppression that constitutes women's experience, along with critiques of patriarchy, sexism, classism, and other realities that dehumanize life. The quests for justice and liberation form central directions in feminist thought. On the global stage, feminist theologians are found worldwide, with particular emphases emerging in relation to the specific contexts and forms of oppression women face. Leading figures are Mary Daly, Rosemary Radford Ruether, Letty Russell, Sallie McFague, Elisabeth Schüssler Fiorenza, Jacquelyn Grant, Elizabeth Johnson, and Mary McClintock Fulkerson.

Narrative Theology

An examination of the relationship between narrative as a form for literary expression and theological reflection has led to the development of narrative theology. Scripture is seen as essentially a narrative of God's relationship to the world, expressed in various literary forms such as narrative, poetry, prophecy, and history. In reaction to modern critical scholarship, narrative theology sought to move beyond the constraints of reason and science to recover what its adherents believe is the essential form of Scripture—narrative. Stories have the power to shape consciousness. Narrative theology does not seek a coherent methodology as much as to use a variety as means to find the relevance of the scriptural narrative for contemporary life. Leading figures are Stanley M. Hauerwas, James William McClendon Jr., George W. Stroup, and Gabriel Fackre.

Postcolonial Theology

Theology has become a dialogue partner with postcolonial theory, which considers the continued impact of European colonization on the societies that were colonized. Postcolonial theology argues that Christianity was intermixed with colonialism and was used to support colonial expansion. European culture was the defining element in the Christianity provided to those who were colonized. The link of imperialism and Christianity meant the Bible was not presented to indigenous cultures for their interpretation but was already translated and interpreted using European categories. Leading figures include R. S. Sugirtharajah (India), Fernando Segovia (Latin America), Kwok Pui-lan (Asia),and Mayra Rivera (Latin America).

Postliberal Theology

This movement is a reaction to liberal theology, which post-liberals believe compromised Christianity to culture in order to try to make the faith relevant to contemporary people and give it a universal appeal. Postliberalism emphasizes the uniqueness of Christianity and its particular place in history. It seeks to have Christian language and tradition shape our human experience so these become the cultural-linguistic world in which we live. Doctrine functions like grammar to guide our use of language for describing the realities of our world and of God. Doctrines or Christian beliefs may be reformed as the church listens and seeks to obey the narrative of the Bible. Leading figures are George Lindbeck, Hans W. Frei, and Stanley M. Hauerwas.

Womanist Theology

Womanist theology is articulated by women of color. Womanist theologians claim their cultural roots, define themselves in relation to them, and embrace their religious traditions as well as their own embodiment. The principle of holism is a guiding factor leading womanist theologians to address issues of race, class, sexuality, and ecology. Daily experience provides the source for theology, which also entails the recognition of the sacred in places where oppression and rejection are found. Liberation from all forms of oppression is corporate in nature. Leading figures are Katie Geneva Cannon, Jacquelyn Grant, Delores Williams, and Emilie Townes.

IX. THE PERSONAL TOUCH

37. INTERESTING TIDBITS ABOUT . . .

Augustine

Augustine attributed his conversion to hearing neighborhood children chanting, "Take and read, take and read," and his turning to the Scriptures at Romans 13:13. He read this verse and responded in this way "For instantly, as the sentence ended, there was infused in my heart something like the light of full certainty and all the gloom of doubt vanished away."*

Dietrich Bonhoeffer

Bonhoeffer was a twin.

Bonhoeffer learned to drive a car in the United States. He failed his driver's examination three times.

John Chrysostom

Chrysostom referred to the New Testament some 11,000 times in his writings but never cited 2 Peter, 2 and 3 John, Jude, or Revelation, since these writings were not part of the New Testament writings circulating in Antioch in the fourth century.

Jonathan Edwards

Edwards liked chocolate.

* Augustine, *Confessions,* 8.12.29 in *Augustine: Confessions and Enchiridion,* ed. and trans. Albert C. Outler, Library of Christian Classics (Philadelphia: The Westminster Press, 1955), 176.

John Knox

Knox spent nineteen months as a galley slave on a French ship.

Martin Luther

Luther married a former nun, Katharina von Bora.

Friedrich Schleiermacher

Asteroid 12694 Schleiermacher is named for Friedrich Schleiermacher.

John Wesley

Wesley was saved from a house fire when he was two years old.

Huldrych Zwingli

Zwingli could play six musical instruments.

38. THEOLOGICAL HUMOR

If theology is the joyful science, there should be room for a good chuckle, even when thinking of very serious theological matters!

A number of examples of humor about theology, theological views, and theologians have circulated through the years. Here are a few:

Augustine

"How, then, shall I respond to him who asks, 'What was God doing *before* he made heaven and earth?' I do not answer, as a certain one is reported to have done facetiously (shrugging off the force of the question). 'He was preparing hell,' he said, 'for those who pry too deep.'"[*]

Karl Barth, Paul Tillich, and Rudolf Bultmann

These three were major theologians of the twentieth century. Here is a joke in which the names are interchangeable.

Karl Barth, Rudolf Bultmann, and Paul Tillich are fishing together on Lake Geneva. They are having a lovely time, smoking their pipes and chatting idly. It's hot, however, and they are getting thirsty. So Barth gets up, steps out of the boat, walks across the water to the shore, gets some beer, and returns. But on such a hot day the beer doesn't last long. Barth tells Tillich, "Your turn, Paul." Tillich gets up, steps out of the boat, walks across the water, and fetches some beer.

It is getting really hot now, and the beer is finished once again. Bultmann is beginning to sweat profusely, so Barth

* Augustine, *Confessions,* 11.12.14 in *Augustine: Confessions and Enchiridion,* ed. and trans. Albert C. Outler, Library of Christian Classics (Philadelphia: The Westminster Press, 1955), 253.

says, "Come on, Rudolf, your turn now." With a slight tremor in his knees, Bultmann gets up, steps out of the boat, and sinks like a stone. Fortunately, he is a good swimmer, and he drags himself back into the boat and sulks at the far end.

Tillich turns to Barth and says, "Do you think we should have told him where the stepping stones are?"

Barth looks at him in astonishment and replies, "What stones?"*

Karl Barth

- Barth was known for his pipe smoking. When Barth was asked about theologians who smoked, he said, "Those who smoke cigarettes are liberals. Those who smoke cigars are conservatives. Those who smoke pipes are just right!"

- "Four days before his death, [Barth] told two friends that he had at last discovered the explanation of the size and number of his books. 'My doctors discovered that my colon was much too long,' he said. 'Now at last I know why there is no end to my volumes on dogmatics.'"†

Paul Tillich

Tillich's theology is highly philosophical and technical in nature. It is also considered not very "personal."

- When Tillich died, he said to God, "Are you the 'ground of being' or 'being itself'? God replied, "Huh?"

- When Tillich died and came in front of Jesus Christ, Christ asked him, "Who do you say that I am?" Tillich replied,

* Adapted from an August 30, 2007, post on The Ironic Catholic blog: http://www.ironiccatholic.com/2007/08/obscure-jokes-about-theology-example-2.html.
† Karl Barth, *Fragments Grave and Gay* (London: Fontana, 1971), 125.

"You are the eschatological manifestation of the ground of our being, the ontological foundation of the context of our very selfhood revealed." And Jesus replied, "What?"

Exorcism

What happens if you don't pay your exorcist?
  You get re-possessed.

Heaven

There are four types of people you will look for in heaven:

- Those who are there and should be there
- Those who are not there and should be there
- Those who you are surprised to see there
- Those who are surprised to see you there!

Philosophy

René Descartes was a seventeenth-century philosopher known as the "Father of Rationalism." To prove his existence, he came up with the Latin phrase Cogito ergo sum, *"I think; therefore I am." If he is thinking and* realizes *he is thinking, then he must exist.*

Descartes was riding in an airplane. A flight attendant asked if he would like a beverage. He replied, "I think not"—and disappeared!

Prayer

A man was falling off a building. He prayed, "Oh God, save me!" Just then he grabbed onto a flagpole sticking out from the side of the building. Then he prayed, "Never mind, Lord. I just grabbed this flagpole!"

Predestination

A major theological debate through the centuries has been about predestination and free will. The Reformed (Presbyterian) tradition has emphasized God's ordaining of events while the Arminian (Methodist) tradition has emphasized human actions.

Once a Presbyterian and a Methodist were walking together. The Methodist tripped and fell. When he got up he said, "I'll have to be more careful next time." As they continued, the Presbyterian tripped and fell. When he got up he said, "Thank God that's over!"

Sin

One of the theological dimensions of sin is our self-centeredness and tendency to focus on ourselves. Sin is when you turn on your computer and do a search on your own name first.

Westminster Shorter Catechism

Question 1 of the Westminster Shorter Catechism asks, "What is man's chief end?" The answer: "Man's chief end is to glorify God and enjoy him forever." When a little boy was asked to answer the first question he responded, "Man's chief end is to glorify God and endure him forever."

39. GOLDEN NUGGETS FROM THEOLOGIANS

Archibald Alexander

"I consider the preaching of the Gospel to be the most honorable and important work in the world."

—Archibald Alexander, "Rightly Dividing the Word of Truth," in *The Princeton Pulpit*, ed. John T. Duffield (New York: Charles Scribner, 1852), 46

William Ames

"Theology is better defined as that good life whereby we live to God than as that happy life whereby we live to ourselves."

—*The Marrow of Theology*, trans. John Dykstra Eusden (Boston: Pilgrim Press, 1968), I.1.8 [p. 78]

"Theology is not a speculative discipline but a practical one."

—*The Marrow of Theology*, I.1.10 [p. 78]

Athanasius

"He, indeed, assumed humanity that we might become God."

—*On the Incarnation* 54, trans. Sister Penelope Lawson, of the Anglican Community of St. Mary the Virgin in Wantage, England

Augustine

"The human will does not attain grace by freedom, but rather freedom by grace."

—*De correptione et gratia* [ET *A Treatise on Rebuke and Grace*], 8.17; Nicene and Post-Nicene Fathers, 5:478

"The reason why these [the bread and wine] are called sacraments is that one thing is seen in them, but something else is understood. That which is seen has bodily appearance; that which is understood has spiritual fruit."

—*Sermon 272,* in *The Later Christian Fathers*, ed. and trans. Henry Bettenson (repr., New York: Oxford University Press, 1972), 244

Karl Barth

When a student asked Barth what the most important discovery he had made through his long life had been, Barth replied, "Jesus loves me this I know, for the Bible tells me so."

—*Fragments Grave and Gay*, trans. Eric Mosbacher (London: Fontana, 1971), 124

"There may be great lawyers, doctors, natural scientists, historians, and philosophers. But there are none other than *little* theologians."

—*Evangelical Theology*, trans. Grover Foley (repr., London: Collins, 1969), 75

"God may speak to us through Russian Communism, a flute concerto, a blossoming shrub, or a dead dog."

—*Church Dogmatics*, eds. G. W. Bromiley and T. F. Torrance, trans. G. W. Bromiley (repr., Edinburgh: T. & T. Clark, 1980), I/1

"Faith is the *condition sine qua non* [condition without which] of theological science. That is to say, faith is the event and history without which no one can become and be a Christian.

—*Evangelical Theolog*, trans. Grover Foley (repr., London: Collins, 1969), 98

"One can *not* speak of God simply by speaking of man in a loud voice."

—*The Word of God and the Word of Man*, trans. Douglas Horton (New York: Harper Torchbooks, 1957), 196

Hendrikus Berkhof

"The authority of the Bible is not the authority of a code but that of a road."

—*Introduction to the Study of Dogmatics*, trans. John Vriend (Grand Rapids: William B. Eerdmans Publishing Co., 1985), 18

Donald G. Bloesch

"The essence of true prayer is heartfelt supplication, bringing before God one's innermost needs and requests in the confident expectation that God will hear and answer."

—*The Struggle of Prayer* (San Francisco: Harper & Row, 1980), 67

Leonardo Boff and Clodovis Boff

"Evangelical conversion requires more than a change of heart; it also requires a liberation of social organization insofar as it produces and reproduces sinful patterns of behavior. This social conversion is brought about through transformative social struggle, with the tactics and strategy suited to bringing about the changes needed. Social sin has to be opposed by social grace, fruit of God's gift and of human endeavor inspired by God."

—*Introducing Liberation Theology*, trans. Paul Burns (Maryknoll, New York: Orbis Books, 1987), 62

Bonaventure and Aquinas

One of Bonaventure's famous friends was St. Thomas Aquinas. Thomas asked him one day where he got all the beautiful things he wrote. St. Bonaventure took his friend by the hand and led him to his desk. Pointing to the large crucifix which always stood on the desk, he said, "Look! It is He Who tells me everything. He is my only Teacher."

—The Ironic Catholic blog, http://ironiccatholic.blogspot.com

Dietrich Bonhoeffer

"We must be ready to allow ourselves to be interrupted by God, who will thwart our plans and frustrate our ways time and again, even daily, by sending people across our path with their demands and requests."

—*Life Together/Prayerbook of the Bible*, ed. Geffrey B. Kelly, trans. Daniel W. Bloesch and James H. Burtness, Dietrich Bonhoeffer Works, vol. 5 (Minneapolis: Fortress Press, 1996), 99

"Death reveals that the world is not as it should be but that it stands in need of redemption. Christ alone is the conquering of death."

—Finkenwalde circular letter, August 15, 1941

"The forgiveness of sins still remains the sole ground of all peace, even where the order of external peace remains preserved in truth and justice."

—"Theology and the World," in *No Rusty Swords: Letters, Lectures, and Notes from the Collected Works* (repr., London: Fontana Library, 1970), 165

"We are silent early in the morning because God should have the first word, and we are silent before going to bed because the last word also belongs to God."

—*Life Together*, 85

"The community of faith does not need brilliant personalities but faithful servants of Jesus and of one another. It does not lack the former, but the latter."

—*Life Together*, 107

José Miguez Bonino

"Theology . . . is not an effort to give a correct understanding of God's attributes or actions but an effort to articulate the action of faith, the shape of praxis conceived and realized in obedience. . . . Theology has to stop explaining the world and to start transforming it. *Orthopraxis*, rather than orthodoxy, becomes the criterion for theology."

—*Doing Theology in a Revolutionary Situation* (repr., Philadelphia: Fortress Press, 1983), 81

St. Brendan

"One of my favorite stories of the old Saints concerns St. Brendan who was given the privilege of preaching to King Brude. The king listened to the sermon with interest as St. Brendan told of Jesus Christ's death and resurrection and the king asked St. Brendan, 'What shall I find if I accept your gospel and become Christ's man?' To which the saint replied: 'If you accept this gospel and become Christ's man, you will stumble on wonder upon wonder, and every wonder true.'"

—John Gladstone, *The Valley of the Verdict* (Toronto: G. R. Welch Company Limited, 1968), 56

Martin Bucer

Theology is the "art of leading a godly life (*scientia vivendi deum*)."

—Martin Bucer, *Martini Buceri: Scripta Anglicana fere omnia* (Basel: Perna, 1577), 563, quoted in Willem van 't Spijker, *Calvin: A Brief Guide to His Life and Thought*, trans. Lyle D. Bierma (Louisville, KY: Westminster John Knox Press, 2009), 131

John Calvin

"Wherever we see the Word of God purely preached and heard, and the sacraments administered according to Christ's institution, there, it is not to be doubted, a church of God exists."

—*Institutes of the Christian Religion* (Philadelphia: Westminster Press, 1960), 4.1.9

"In the Gospel we have an open revelation of God."

—*Commentary on 2 Corinthians 3:18* (Calvin's New Testament
    Commentaries, 10:49)

"God is comprehended in Christ alone."

—*Institutes* 2.6.4

"Faith is the principal work of the Holy Spirit."

—*Institutes* 3.1.4

"But we are free to help by prayer even utterly foreign
and unknown persons, however great the distance that
separates them from us."

—*Institutes* 3.20.39

"For what is the sum total of the gospel except that we
all, being slaves of sin and death, are released and freed
through the redemption which is in Christ Jesus."

—*Institutes* 4.11.1

"The faithful are not free from despair, for it enters into
their souls; but . . . there is no reason why they should
indulge despair; on the contrary, they ought courageously
and firmly to resist it. . . . The remedy is, immediately to
flee to God and to complain of this misery, so that he may
succor and raise up those who are thus fallen."

—*Commentary on Lamentations* 3:18

"But we live with a quiet mind and go on to meet death
without hesitation because a better hope is laid up for us."

—*Commentary on 2 Corinthians* 5:6

Katie Geneva Cannon

"Transformative grace begins and ends with God's union with humanity. This union is created by God, sustained by the love of Christ, and made continuous, morning by morning, by the Holy Spirit. We have been gripped by God's Spirit, touched by divine love, and redeemed by grace. God has each of us in God's embrace. All in all, transformative grace functions for hard-pressed Christian people on a shrinking globe as a mandate for thankful, creative living."

—"Transformative Grace," in *Feminist and Womanist Essays in Reformed Dogmatics*, ed. Amy Plantinga Pauw and Serene Jones. Columbia Series in Reformed Theology (Louisville, KY: Westminster John Knox Press, 2006), 151

Catherine of Siena

Christ's command to her: "What you cannot do for me, you should do for your neighbor."

—Justo L. González, ed., *The Westminster Dictionary of Theologians* (Louisville, KY: Westminster John Knox Press, 2006), 83

Ronald S. Cole-Turner

"The ascension is a crucial moment of revelation, showing us the larger story of God's loving action. It is a reminder that our lives are caught up in something far more grand than we can imagine."

—Commentary on Acts 1:1–11, in *Feasting on the Word*, ed. David L. Bartlett and Barbara Brown Taylor (Louisville, KY: Westminster John Knox Press, 2009), 6:502

David S. Cunningham

"Sunday is the day that is supposed to put us in mind of Easter—and not just for that day but for our entire lives."

—*Friday, Saturday, Sunday: Literary Meditations on Suffering, Death, and New Life* (Louisville, KY: Westminster John Knox Press, 2007), 129

James Denney

"The correlative of grace is gratitude."

—*The Expositor* (February 1904), 160

Avery Dulles

"Faith cannot do the work of science, nor can the Bible function as a textbook of astronomy or biology."

—*The Craft of Theology: From Symbol to System* (New York: Crossroad, 1992), 139

"Theology is a reflection upon faith from within the commitment of faith."

—*The Craft of Theology: From Symbol to System* (New York: Crossroad, 1992), 168

Evagrius of Pontus

"If you are a theologian, pray truly; and if you pray truly, you are a theologian."

—Kathleen Norris, *Amazing Grace: A Vocabulary of Faith* (New York: Riverhead Books, 1998), 359

Peter Taylor Forsyth

"The unity of the Bible is organic, total, vital, evangelical; it is not merely harmonious, balanced, statuesque. It is not the form of symmetry but the spirit of reconciliation."

—"Evangelical Churches and Higher Criticism," in *The Gospel and Authority: A P. T. Forsyth Reader*, ed. Marvin W. Anderson (Minneapolis: Augsburg Publishing House, 1971), 37

"Prayer is not only a necessity of faith, it is faith itself in action."

—*The Soul of Prayer* (Vancouver, British Columbia: Regent College Publishing, 2002), 74

"Christ is the condensation of history."

—*The Work of Christ* (London: Fontana, 1965), 119

Charles Hodge

"I am not afraid to say that a new idea never originated in this Seminary."

—*Proceedings Connected with Semi-Centennial Commemoration of the Rev. Professor Charles Hodge, D.D., L.L.D. in the Theological Seminary at Princeton, N.J., April 24, 1872* (New York: Anson D. F. Randolph, 1872), 52

Kendra G. Hotz

"God claims us, not because we are worthy, but because we cannot be."

—Commentary on 1 Samuel 2:18–20, 26, in *Feasting on the Word*, ed. David L. Bartlett and Barbara Brown Taylor (Louisville, KY: Westminster John Knox Press, 2009) 5:148

Irenaeus

"Our Lord Jesus Christ, the word of God, of his boundless love, became what we are that he might make us what he himself is."

—*Against Heresies* , praef. 5 in *The Early Christian Fathers*, ed. and trans. Henry Bettenson (New York: Oxford University Press, 1969), 77

Robert Clyde Johnson

"When we read a biography of Julius Caesar, or of Winston Churchill, nothing more is demanded of us than a reasonable ability to understand what the words mean. But this is not true when we read about Jesus Christ. He demands not only the insight of our minds, but also the allegiance of our lives. And correct understanding *of* him depends upon this allegiance *to* him. It can come in no other way. Here to 'understand' means to 'stand under,' to give him our complete allegiance. . . . The cross, beyond all else, can be 'understood' only as we 'stand under' it, or only as—and in so far as—it becomes an ever-present reality in our deepest experience."

—*The Meaning of Christ,* The Layman's Theological Library (Philadelphia: The Westminster Press, 1958), 19, 61

Serene Jones

"The image of theological dramas suggests that doctrines function like loose but nonetheless definitive scripts that persons of faith perform; doctrines are the dramas in which we live out our lives. The image of landscape suggests that doctrines construct an imagistic and conceptual terrain within which people of faith locate and interpret their lives and the world around them. This terrain is marked by signposts that classical theology identified as the central doctrines of the faith."

—*Feminist Theory and Christian Theology: Cartographies of Grace.* Guides to Theological Inquiry (Minneapolis: Augsburg Fortress, 2000), 17

"Christian doctrine is not a world of strict principles and static beliefs. Rather, doctrines are lived, imaginative landscapes, which persons of faith inhabit and within which their Christian identity is shaped."

—*Feminist Theory and Christian Theology*, 50

Eberhard Jüngel

"To believe in God the Holy Spirit means to acknowledge Jesus Christ as our future."

—*God as the Mystery of the World*, trans. Darrell L. Guder (Grand Rapids: Wm. B. Eerdmans Publishing Co., 1983), 388

David H. Kelsey

"Christians learn to imagine the world according to the paradigm exemplified by their creeds, by their liturgies, by their Scriptures interpreted as a canonical whole, and most decisively by the Synoptic Gospels' narrative rendering of Jesus' personal identity. Among other things, Christians learn to imagine the world according to that paradigm as a world redeemed."

—*Imagining Redemption* (Louisville, KY: Westminster John Knox Press, 2005), 104

Hans Küng

"Cross and resurrection form the centre of Christian faith."

—*Christianity*, trans. John W. Bowden (New York: Crossroad, 1998), 49

"Christian theology to a considerable extent is constantly detective work, often an extremely absorbing and exhausting work of discovery."

—*On Being a Christian*, trans. Edward Quinn (Garden City, NY: Doubleday, 1976), 129–30

Martin Luther

"But the glory of our God is precisely that for our sakes he comes down to the very depths, into human flesh, into the bread, into our mouth, our heart, our bosom."

—*Word and Sacrament*, ed. Robert H. Fischer, trans. Helmet T. Lehmann (Philadelphia: Fortress Press, 1961), 37:72

"Anything on which your heart relies and depends, I say, that is really your God."

—*Large Catechism* in *The Book of Concord,* ed. Robert Kolb and Timothy J. Wengert, trans. Charles Arand, et. al. (Minneapolis: Fortress Press, 2000), 386

"The Bible is alive, it speaks to me; it has feet, it runs after me; it has hands, it lays hold of me."

—*The Table Talk of Martin Luther*, ed. Thomas S. Kepler (Mineolo, New York: Dover, 2005), 197

Martin Marty

"A theological lecture talks *about* God. A sermon *offers* God."

—Commentary on Luke 24:1–12 , in *Feasting on the Word*, ed. David L. Bartlett and Barbara Brown Taylor (Louisville, KY: Westminster John Knox Press, 2009), 6:348

Daniel L. Migliore

"Love is the new way to be human with and for others supremely embodied in Jesus Christ and empowered in us by the Holy Spirit."

—*Faith Seeking Understanding*, 2nd ed. (Grand Rapids: Wm. B. Eerdmans Publishing Co., 2004), 161

"The Bible has a central story; it is more like an epic drama than an encyclopedia."

—*The Power of God and the Gods of Power* (Louisville, KY: Westminster John Knox Press, 2008), 40

Nathan D. Mitchell

"[In liturgy] time is defined by meaning instead of its duration."

—Commentary on 2 Corinthians 5:20b–6:10, in *Feasting on the Word,* ed. David L. Bartlett and Barbara Brown Taylor (Louisville, KY: Westminster John Knox Press, 2009), 6:18

Jürgen Moltmann

"Life is communication in communion."

—*God in Creation*, trans. Margaret Kohl (San Francisco: Harper & Row, 1985), 3

"The experience of God deepens the experiences of life. It does not reduce them, for it awakens the unconditional Yes to life. The more I love God the more gladly I exist. The more immediately and wholly I exist, the more I sense the living God, the inexhaustible well of life, and life's eternity."

—*The Spirit of Life: A Universal Affirmation*, trans. Margaret Kohl (Minneapolis: Fortress Press, 1993), 98

"The real point is not to spread the church but to spread the kingdom."

—*The Church in the Power of the Spirit*, trans. Margaret Kohl (New York: Harper & Row, 1977), 11

Martha Moore-Keish

"Who is the God we encounter in prayer? God is source, goal, and companion in prayer, the Holy Trinity that envelops us as we pray, drawing us (if we open ourselves to it) into ever deeper communion with God. True prayer is thus participation in God."

—*Christian Prayer for Today* (Louisville, KY: Westminster John Knox Press, 2009), 11

"Prayer gives voice to all of these aspects of our human selves: our pain in the present, our memories of the past, and our hopes for the future. In this way, though prayer is not directed toward ourselves, it is profoundly about ourselves—our *true* selves, fashioned in the image of God and called into communion with that One who is behind, beside, and before us."

—*Christian Prayer for Today*, 28

H. Richard Niebuhr

The omnipotence of God is not like the power of the world which is in his power. His power is made perfect in weakness and he exercises sovereignty more through crosses than through thrones."

—*The Meaning of Revelation*. Library of Theological Ethics (Louisville, KY: Westminster John Knox Press, 2006), 98

Reinhold Niebuhr

"The Kingdom of God as it *has come* in Christ means a disclosure of the meaning of history but not the full realization of that meaning. That is anticipated in the Kingdom which *is to come*, that is, in the culmination of history."

—*The Nature and Destiny of Man*, 2 vols. (repr., New York: Charles Scribner's Sons, 1964), 2:288

Johannes Oecolampadius

"For all of Scripture looks to Christ as its target so to speak."

—Commentary on Isaiah 2:1, in *Dictionary of Major Biblical Interpreters*, ed. Donald K. McKim (Downers Grove, IL: InterVarsity Press, 2007), 783

Origen

"We suppose that the goodness of God will restore the whole creation to unity in the end, through his Christ, when his enemies have been subdued and overcome."

—*On First Principles* I. 6.1, in *The Early Christian Fathers*, ed. and trans. Henry Bettenson (New York: Oxford University Press, 1969), 256

Heinrich Ott

"In Christ's resurrection we know 'God has the power to create a new beginning out of the nothingness of absolute meaninglessness.'"

—*Die Antwort des Glaubens: Systematische Theologie in 50 Artikeln* (Berlin: Kreuz Verlag, 1981), 226f, quoted in John E. Wilson, *Introduction to Modern Theology: Trajectories in the German Tradition* (Louisville, KY: Westminster John Knox Press, 2007), 268 n. 97

"'All communication of God rests on pure grace alone.'"

—*Apologetik des Glaubens: Grundprobleme einer dialogischen Fundamentaltheologie* (Darmstadt: Wissenschaftliche Buchgesellschaft, c1994), 207, quoted in Wilson, *Introduction to Modern Theology*, 267 n. 92

Wolfhart Pannenberg

"In the coming of Jesus the future of God and his reign that Jesus proclaimed were present by anticipation. In person, then, Jesus was a sign of the coming divine rule, so that by him and in fellowship with him people may be assured even now of their participation in the future salvation of this rule."

—*Systematic Theology*, trans. Geoffrey W. Bromiley, 3 vols. (Grand Rapids: Wm. B. Eerdmans Publishing Co., 1998), 3:435

Robert S. Paul

"A church shows itself to be authentically the Church only when it acts in a truly catholic way, i.e., when it shows itself representatively or corporately to belong to the Church Universal."

—*The Church in Search of Its Self* (Grand Rapids: Wm. B. Eerdmans Publishing Co., 1972), 290

"The vocation of the Church *is* to become 'Christ in community,' but . . . when a community represents itself as having already achieved the perfection to which it is called, it actually reveals how imperfectly it has understood its own gospel. The Church is *en route* to the Kingdom."

—*The Church in Search of Its Self,* 302

Amy Plantinga Pauw

"Christian existence is a life-long tutorial in the gracious ways of God with us and in the paths we are to follow toward God and neighbor. Scripture is a primary resource for this tutorial."

—"The Holy Spirit and Scripture," in *The Lord and Giver of Life: Perspectives on Constructive Pneumatology*, ed. David H. Jensen (Louisville, KY: Westminster John Knox Press, 2008), 29

"As the body of Christ in the world, the church is a broken and diseased body, mirroring the ills and divisions of the larger society. Yet it remains a mysteriously powerful channel of God's grace to us. The church is a nursery of piety, where Christians are schooled by worship, teaching, and discipline into deeper communion with Christ and each other."

—"The Graced Infirmity of the Church," in *Feminist and Womanist Essays in Reformed Dogmatics*, ed. Amy Plantinga Pauw and Serene Jones, Columbia Series in Reformed Theology (Louisville, KY: Westminster John Knox Press, 2006), 191

Jaroslav Pelikan

"Tradition is the living faith of the dead; traditionalism is the dead faith of the living."

—*The Vindication of Tradition* (New Haven: Yale University Press, 1984), 65

William Perkins

"Theologie is the science of living blessedly forever."

—"*A* Golden Chaine," in *The Workes of William Perkins*, 3 vols. (Cambridge: John Legate, 1616–1618), I:11

"When a crosse cometh, it is a hard thing to be patient; but wee must draw our seules thereunto by consideration of Gods especiall prouidence."

—"An Exposition of the Creede," in *The Workes of William Perkins*, I:158

Eugene Peterson

"The theologians' task is to train our thinking, our imagination, our understanding to *begin* with God, not ourselves."

—foreword to *The Soul of Prayer* by P. T. Forsyth (Vancouver, British Columbia: Regent College Publishing, 2002), 3

William C. Placher

"Jesus Christ united humanity with divinity, thereby transforming what it is to be human. We human beings turn away and separate ourselves from God, but in Christ divinity is reunited with humanity. In our culture, where many people are told, explicitly or implicitly, that they are worthless, Christian faith must declare all the more boldly that the humanity of every single human being has been united to God in Christ."

—*Jesus the Savior: The Meaning of Jesus Christ for Christian Faith* (Louisville, KY: Westminster John Knox Press, 2001), 16

"In the case of the resurrection, it seems crucial to Christian faith to believe that something took place that was radically different from what usually happens to people after they die: thanks to an action of God, Jesus, who had died, yet lived. Without that, the Gospels' whole sense of Jesus' identity breaks down."

—*Jesus the Savior*, 89

Edward Schillebeeckx

"The kingdom of God is not an unearthly other world, but the completion of the restoration of this world, our world which is out of joint. Therefore the contemporary experience of men and women who as followers of Jesus place fragmentary signs of the kingdom of God in this world, our world that is out of joint, is also the foundation for a firm hope of a kingdom of God grounded in Jesus that will one day be completed."

—*Church: The Human Story of God*, trans. John Bowden (New York: Crossroad, 1993), 133

Friedrich Schleiermacher

"Conceptions of doctrine are developed . . . through continual reflection on Christian self-consciousness."

—*Brief Outline on the Study of Theology as a Field of Study: Revised Translation of the 1811 and 1830 Editions, with Essays and Notes by Terrence N. Tice,* trans. Terrence N. Tice, 3rd ed. (Louisville, KY: Westminster John Knox Press, 2011), §177

"The Redeemer assumes the believers into the fellowship of His unclouded blessedness, and this is His reconciling activity."

—*The Christian Faith*, trans. of the 2nd German edition, ed. H. R. Mackintosh and J. S. Stewart (Edinburgh: T. & T. Clark, 1928), 431

Alexander Schmemann

"For through the Cross, joy came into the whole world."

—*For the Life of the World* (St. Vladimir Press, 1998), 55

Dorothee Soelle

"God is not in heaven; he is hanging on the cross."

—*Suffering* , trans. Everett R. Kalin (Philadelphia: Fortress Press, 1975), 148

Kathryn Tanner

"The incarnation is not, then, to be identified with one moment of Jesus' life, his birth, in contradistinction from his ministry, death and resurrection. The incarnation is, to the contrary, the underlying given that makes all that Jesus does and suffers purifying, healing and elevating."

—*Jesus, Humanity and the Trinity: A Brief Systematic Theology* (repr., Minneapolis: Fortress Press, 2003), 28

Barbara Brown Taylor

"Faith, by definition, is radical trust in what God is doing, even when the divine mode of operation is far from clear."

—Commentary on John 1:6–8, 19–28, in *Feasting on the Word*, ed. David L. Bartlett and Barbara Brown Taylor (Louisville, KY: Westminster John Knox Press, 2008), 1:71

"Salvation happens every time someone with a key uses it to open a door he could lock instead."

— *Leaving Church: A Memoir of Faith* (San Francisco: Harper San Francisco, 2006), 115

"In the Bible, human beings experience God's salvation when peace ends war, when food follows famine, when health supplants sickness and freedom trumps oppression. *Salvation* is a word for the divine spaciousness that comes to human beings in all the tight places where their lives are at risk, regardless of how they got there or whether they know God's name. Sometimes it comes as an extended human hand and sometimes as a bolt from the blue, but either way it opens a door in what looked for all the world like a wall. This is the way of life, and God alone knows how it works."

—*Leaving Church,* 226

Tertullian

"The flesh feeds on the body and blood of Christ that the soul may be fattened on God."

—*On the Resurrection of the Body*, 8, in *The Early Christian Fathers*, ed. and trans. Henry Bettenson (New York: Oxford University Press, 1969), 148

Helmut Thielicke

"Faith can be described only as a movement of flight, flight away from myself and toward the great possibilities of God."

—*Theological Ethics: Foundations*, ed. William H. Lazareth (Grand Rapids: Wm. B. Eerdmans Publishing Co., 1979), 283

August Tholuck

"The story is told that the once famous Professor Tholuck of Halle used to visit the rooms of his students and press them with the question, 'Brother, how are things in your heart?' How do things stand with you yourself?—not with your ears, not with your head, not with your forensic ability, not with your industriousness (although all that is also appropriate to being a theologian). In biblical terms the question is precisely, 'How are things with your *heart*?' It is a question very properly addressed to every young and old theologian."

—Karl Barth, *Evangelical Theology*, trans. Grover Foley (repr., London: Collins, 1969), 81

Paul Tillich

"The object of theology is what concerns us ultimately. Only those propositions are theological which deal with their object in so far as it can become a matter of ultimate concern for us."

—*Systematic Theology,* 3 vols. (repr., Chicago: University of Chicago Press, 1967), 1:12

"The task of theology is mediation, mediation between the eternal criterion of truth as it is manifest in the picture of Jesus as the Christ and the changing experiences of individuals and groups, their varying questions and their categories of perceiving reality."

—*The Protestant Era* (Chicago: University of Chicago Press, 1957), ix

Benjamin B. Warfield

"May [God] give us his Holy Spirit to sanctify us wholly and enable us when we close our eyes in our long sleep to open them at once, not in terrified pain in torment, but in the soft, sweet light of Paradise, safe in the arms of Jesus."

—"The Christian's Attitude toward Death," in *Princeton Sermons* (New York: Fleming H. Revell Co., 1893), 337

John Wesley

"In the evening I went very unwillingly to a society in Aldersgate Street, where one was reading Luther's preface to the *Epistle to the Romans*. About a quarter before nine, while he was describing the change which God works in the heart through faith in Christ, I felt my heart strangely warmed. I felt I did trust in Christ, Christ alone for salvation; and an assurance was given me that He had taken away *my* sins, even *mine*, and saved *me* from the law of sin and death."

—*The Journal of John Wesley* (May 24, 1738)

Ralph W. Wood

"We are ensouled bodies and embodied souls."

—Commentary on Philippians 3:17–4:1, in *Feasting on the Word*, ed. David L. Bartlett and Barbara Brown Taylor (Louisville, KY: Westminster John Knox Press, 2009), 6:66

Suzanne Woolston-Bossert

"Perhaps the extra day after Good Friday was needed because God was plunged into mourning just like the rest of us."

—Commentary on Lamentations 3:1–9, 19–24, in *Feasting on the Word*, ed. David L. Bartlett and Barbara Brown Taylor (Louisville, KY: Westminster John Knox Press, 2009), 6:310

40. A PERSONAL CREDO

Sometimes statements of theological belief can use very formal structures and language. Other times they directly engage matters of direct, personal concern.

Here are excerpts of a personal statement of belief from German theologian Dorothee Soelle (1929–2003):

> I believe in God, who didn't create the world finished like a thing that is always the same . . . [,] who supports the protest of the living and the change of all conditions through our work and through our politics.
>
> I believe in Jesus Christ . . . [,] who worked for the change of all conditions and focused on root causes. . . . Every day I am afraid that He died in vain because he is buried in our churches, because we have betrayed his revolution in obedience and fear of authorities. . . . [He] rises from the dead in our life so we can become free from prejudices and arrogance, from fear and hatred and drive his revolution toward his reign.
>
> I believe in the Spirit that came into this world with Jesus to the community of all nations and our responsibility for what becomes of our earth: a valley full of lamentation . . . or the city of God.
>
> I believe in the just peace realizable in the possibility of a meaningful life for all people in the future of this world, God's world. Amen.[*]

* Dorothee Soelle, "Justice Is the Foundation of Peace" (address given on the occasion of the Evangelical church day, Frankfurt, June 15, 2003), http://portland.indymedia.org/en/2003/12/276085.shtml.

41. LAST WORDS

Martin Luther (1483–1546)

"On the night of February 18 [1546] he died. Both of the friends who were with him asked the dying Luther if he would remain steadfast and intended to die in Christ and the teaching he himself had preached. Luther replied with a clear and audible: *Ja* ('Yes'). This was his last word."[*]

James Ussher (1581–1656)

He died at one o'clock on March 21 at the age of 75. His last words were reported as "O Lord forgive me, especially my sins of omission."

John Wesley (1703–1791)

According to tradition, Wesley's last words were "Best of all, God is with us."

Karl Barth (1886–1968)

On the last night of his life, December 9, 1968, Karl Barth spoke by telephone with his friend of sixty years, Eduard Thurneysen. Eberhard Busch records: "They talked about the gloomy world situation. Then Barth said, 'But keep your chin up! Never mind! 'He will reign!'"[†]

[*] Albrecht Beutel, "Luther's Life," in *The Cambridge Companion to Martin Luther*, ed. Donald K. McKim (New York: Cambridge University Press, 2003), 18.

[†] Eberhard Busch, *Karl Barth: His Life from Letters and Autobiographical Texts* (Philadelphia: Fortress Press, 1976), 498.

X. GOING ON FROM HERE

42. TEN LEADING LATIN PHRASES IN THEOLOGY

The first theologian to write in Latin was Tertullian. In the Western church, Latin was the ecclesiastical language, and so important theological works were written in this language. A number of Latin phrases are still used among theologians today who do not write in Latin. Here are some important ones.

Analogia entis

Meaning "analogy of being," this term for the relationship of God the Creator to humans as creatures means it is legitimate to use analogy as a way for finite humans to speak of the infinite God.

Analogia fidei

This term, which means "analogy of faith," refers to a view stressed by Protestants that individual Christian doctrines should be understood in light of the whole of Christian faith and that places in Scripture that are obscure should be understood in light of the places in Scripture that are clearer.

Credo ut intelligam / fides quaerens intellectum

These phrases, which mean "I believe in order that I might understand" and "Faith seeking understanding," describe an approach to theology in which one begins in faith in what God has said and done and then moves on to seek further understanding of God by the use of all other resources.

Ex opere operato

Meaning "from the work done," this phrase from Roman Catholic theology teaches that a sacrament has an effect when it is a valid sacrament of the church and that this effect does not depend upon the moral virtue of the one who administers it.

Extra ecclesiam nulla salus

This phrase from the early church theologian Cyprian (d. 258) means, "Outside the church there is no salvation."

Fides ex auditu

Based on Romans 10:17 and emphasized especially by Protestants, this phrase, which means "faith from hearing," stresses Christian preaching as the primary means by which Christian faith is spread and received.

Gloria Patri

An ancient ascription of praise to the Holy Trinity often set to music or spoken in worship that begins, "Glory be to the Father, and to the Son, and to the Holy Spirit."

Mea culpa, mea maxima culpa

An expression of sorrow for sin or contrition, traditionally used in the Roman Catholic tradition as an expression of the desire for repentance, it means "my sin, my great sin."

Simul justus et peccator

Meaning "at the same time righteous and a sinner," this phrase is associated with Luther and his view of justification by faith. The believer is righteous in God's sight because of Jesus Christ while also a sinner, since sin is part of Christian experience.

Theologia gloriae / theologia crucis

These terms, which mean "theology of glory" and "theology of the cross," respectively, are associated with Luther. *Theologia gloriae* describes the speculative, scholastic theology that emphasizes God's glorious attributes; *theologia crucis* stresses the weakness and scandal of the cross of Christ.

43. TEN GREAT GERMAN WORDS IN THEOLOGY

Many of the most prominent theologians have written in German. As a result, a number of German words have become part of the language of theology. Here are some prominent ones.[*]

das Abendmahl (Lord's Supper; Eucharist)

die Auferstehung (resurrection)

die Erbsünde (original sin)

die Erlösung (salvation)

der Gott (God)

die Heilsgeschichte (salvation history)

der Herr (Lord)

die Offenbarung (revelation)

die Rechtfertigung (justification)

die Taufe (baptism)

---

[*] Two helpful resources are J. D. Manton, *Introduction to Theological German: A Beginner's Course for Theological Students*, 2nd ed. (Grand Rapids: Wm. B. Eerdmans Publishing Co., 1973); and Helmut W. Ziefle, *Modern Theological German: A Reader and Dictionary* (Grand Rapids: Baker Books, 1997).

44. A BRIEF LIST OF RESOURCES FOR THEOLOGICAL STUDY

Reference Works

Cross, F. L., and E. A. Livingstone, eds. *The Oxford Dictionary of the Christian Church*. 3rd ed. Oxford: Oxford University Press, 1997.

Dryness, William A., and Veli-Matti Kärkkäinen, eds. *Global Dictionary of Theology: A Resource for the Worldwide Church*. Downers Grove, IL: InterVarsity Press, 2008.

González, Justo L., ed. *The Westminster Dictionary of Theologians*. Translated by Suzanne E. Hoeferkamp Segovia. Louisville, KY: Westminster John Knox Press, 2006.

McKim, Donald K. *The Westminster Dictionary of Theological Terms*. Louisville, KY: Westminster John Knox Press, 1996.

Creeds and Confessions

Campbell, Ted. *Christian Confessions: A Historical Introduction*. Louisville, KY: Westminster John Knox Press, 1996.

Leith, John H. *Creeds of the Churches: A Reader in Christian Doctrine from the Bible to the Present*. Louisville, KY: Westminster John Knox Press, 1983.

Pelikan, Jaroslav, and Valerie R. Hotchkiss, eds. *Creeds and Confessions of Faith in the Christian Tradition*. 4 vols. New Haven, CT: Yale University Press, 2003.

Schaff, Philip. *The Creeds of Christendom: With a History and Critical Notes*. Revised by David S. Schaff. Reprint, Grand Rapids: Baker Book House, 1985.

Histories of Theology

González, Justo L. *A History of Christian Thought.* 3 vols. Nashville: Abingdon Press, 1970–1975.

Olson, Roger E. *The Story of Christian Theology: Twenty Centuries of Tradition and Reform.* Downers Grove, IL: InterVarsity Press, 1999.

Pelikan, Jaroslav. *The Christian Tradition.* 5 vols. Chicago: University of Chicago Press, 1971–1989.

Placher, William C. *A History of Christian Theology: An Introduction.* Philadelphia: Westminster Press, 1983.

Introductions to Theology

Berkhof, Hendrikus. *Introduction to the Study of Dogmatics.* Translated by John Vriend. Grand Rapids: Wm. B. Eerdmans Publishing Co., 1985.

Chopp, Rebecca S., and Mark Lewis Taylor, eds. *Reconstructing Christian Theology.* Minneapolis: Fortress Press, 1994.

González, Justo L., and Zaida Maldonado Pérez. *An Introduction to Christian Theology.* Nashville: Abingdon Press, 1999.

Hodgson, Peter C., and Robert H. King, eds. *Christian Theology: An Introduction to Its Traditions and Tasks.* Minneapolis: Fortress Press, 1994.

Jones, Serene, and Paul Lakeland, eds. *Constructive Theology: A Contemporary Approach to Classical Themes.* Minneapolis: Fortress Press, 2005.

McGrath, Alister E. *Christian Theology: An Introduction.* Malden, MA: Blackwell, 2001.

Migliore, Daniel L. *Faith Seeking Understanding: An Introduction to Christian Theology.* 2nd ed. Grand Rapids: Wm. B. Eerdmans Publishing Co., 2004.

Placher, William C., ed. *Essentials of Christian Theology.* Louisville, KY: Westminster John Knox Press, 2003.

Theologians

Ford, David F., ed. *The Modern Theologians: An Introduction to Christian Theology in the Twentieth Century*. 2nd ed. Cambridge, MA: Blackwell, 1997.

Marty, Martin E., and Dean G. Peerman, eds. *A Handbook of Christian Theologians*. Enlarged ed. Nashville: Abingdon Press, 1984.

McEnhill, Peter, and George Newlands. *Fifty Key Christian Thinkers*. Routledge Key Guides. New York: Routledge, 2004.

A FINAL WORD

FREELY YOU HAVE RECEIVED

I have tried to open some theological windows in these chapters, and I hope these first steps in theology have been both interesting and useful. Most of all, I hope they have whetted your appetite to delve further into the study of Christian theology—to go beyond this "down and dirty" guide!

There is much more to question, consider, learn, and bring into one's life by way of theological study. The benefits will be many! And the joy will be in the journey.

Through it all, none of us will ever really "arrive" as a theologian. We will always be amateurs. Yet we push on to explore the great treasures of Christian theology, and beyond those to obtain the "riches and wisdom and knowledge of God" (Rom. 11:33).

We do it along with others who are also on a theological journey, in the academy or the church. We share theological reflection as both a communal and a personal calling.

We do it all out of gratitude for the riches of God's glory and grace in Jesus Christ (Eph. 1:7; 3:16).

What we learn, we share.

Theologian Martin Rumscheidt was the last Canadian to study under Karl Barth. When Barth returned from a trip to the United States in the winter term of 1961–1962, he received his students at a gathering.

Rumscheidt wrote: "I was to leave for home a week later, and felt sad at having to say what I thought was my final farewell. (Actually my wife and I met him again in 1964.) In any case, I managed to thank him for the immense enrichment, the encouragement and the joy, he had given me. He stood facing me in his black corduroy jacket, his glasses on the tip of his nose and his hair happily tousled. He put both hands on my shoulders, gave them a squeeze and said: 'Freely you have received, freely give.'"*

This is a word for us as theologians, no matter what "stage" we are in. We receive and we give. This is inherent in the nature of living theology itself. It is our task—and our joy!

---

* H. Martin Rumscheidt, from a memorial service for Karl Barth, University of Toronto, December 19, 1968. In Karl Barth, *Fragments Grave and Gay* (London: Fontana, 1971), 127.